TALES OF THE
GYPSY
DRESSMAKER

Thelma Madine

HARPER

HARPER

An imprint of HarperCollins*Publishers*
77–85 Fulham Palace Road,
Hammersmith, London W6 8JB

www.harpercollins.co.uk

First published by HarperCollins*Publishers* 2012
This edition published 2012
1 3 5 7 9 10 8 6 4 2

© Thelma Madine 2012

Edited by Caragh McKay

Thelma Madine asserts the moral right to be
identified as the author of this work

A catalogue record of this book is
available from the British Library

ISBN 978-0-00-745696-3

Printed and bound in Great Britain by
Clays Ltd, St Ives plc

FSC™ is a ~~non-profit international organisation established to~~ promote
the respons~~ible management of the world's forests. Products ca~~rrying the
FSC label a~~re independently certified to assure consumers that t~~hey come
from f~~orests that are managed to meet the social, economic~~ and

Find ~~out more about HarperCollins and the environment~~ at

FIFE COUNCIL LIBRARIES	
HJ315947	
Askews & Holts	09-Jan-2013
920MAD	£7.99
BIOG	BK

I'd like to dedicate this book to the travelling community.

You let me into your world and in turn helped me to understand a little bit of your culture. You opened my eyes to the prejudices you face daily. You helped put me where I am today.

Contents

Prologue

The Pineapple and the Palm Tree

'I want you to make me a wedding dress like no one's ever seen before.'

'OK,' I said, looking at the slim, blonde gypsy girl standing in front of me. 'Have you got any ideas of the kind of dress you'd like?'

She'd made an appointment to come into my shop, Nico, in the centre of Liverpool, so I was expecting her. I was also expecting her request – all my traveller girls want to stand out, determined that their dress will be the biggest and the best, or both.

'I want to be a palm tree,' she said.

'And I'm going to be a pineapple,' piped up the girl who was with her and who I realised straight away was her younger sister, and one of the most enthusiastic bridesmaids I'd ever met. They were both pretty kids and I knew just by looking at them that they were from Rathkeale, the very wealthy gypsy community in Ireland. In Rathkeale the night-before outfits are just as important as the wedding dress. And these two were going all out.

'A palm tree for the bride and a pineapple for the bridesmaid,' I said, looking from one to the other. They were looking at me as though they had just asked me to make a wedding gown like Kate Middleton's, their faces were dead straight, like any anxious bride and bridesmaid, determined that they had to look just right on the Big Day. 'Yeah,' I said, 'we can do that, no problem.'

'Will anyone else have a dress like that?' asked the young girl. 'She's really worried that there will be another bride who wants the same thing as her,' she said, touching her sister's arm, before turning to look at me again.

'Oh, I think she'll be safe with that one,' I said, smiling at them.

I looked down at my sketchbook and started drawing.

Introduction

Now, the first thing everyone asks when they meet me is: are you a gypsy? So now's my chance to put the record straight: no, I am not a gypsy. What I am is a woman from Liverpool who makes and designs wedding dresses. It just so happens that the people who have made my dresses some of the most recognised in the world are gypsies. And that's why I'm now known, from Aberdeen to Auckland, as the Gypsy Dressmaker.

Nothing could have prepared me for the dramas that I have experienced since I started working with gypsies about fifteen years ago – and, believe me, what you've seen on TV is only the half of it.

And that's one of the reasons that I was so keen to write this book – fans of *Big Fat Gypsy Weddings* are constantly asking me to tell them more about me and *my* gypsy stories. Because, beyond the cameras, since I was welcomed into the traveller community many years ago, I have been lucky enough to get a rare insight into what really goes on in their world and to share in their secrets and dreams, their highs and lows and, of course, their laughter. And, honestly, there has been a hell of a lot of that over the years.

The other thing that people are forever asking is: how did you end up working with gypsies in the first place? Well, I suppose it was a coincidence, but you could say that it was a twist of fate. You know, in the way that my mum used to say things like, 'Everything happens for a reason,' or 'What's for you won't go by you.'

It was in 1996, when I had my dressmaker's stall in Paddy's Market in Liverpool, that my first traveller customer approached me. I didn't even know she was a gypsy. I did realise, though, that there was something different about her because she looked very, very young. Too young, in fact, to ask me a strange question like 'Can you make *Gone With the Wind* dresses?'

I mean, it's not your run-of-the-mill request, is it? And it's not the kind of thing that I imagine most dressmakers are normally asked for. The funny thing is, what that gypsy girl couldn't have known that day, when she looked at all the ivory and white christening and Communion robes I had hanging up, was that that great 1930s film about Scarlett O'Hara and the American Civil War was one of the main reasons I wanted to be a seamstress in the first place. Since I was a little girl I had watched that movie a thousand times. And yet, up until then, I had never thought to actually make *Gone With the Wind* dresses.

So the idea that the girl had in her mind for how she wanted to dress her kids, and the kinds of dresses that I wanted to make, came together at Paddy's that day and started what would eventually become a phenomenon.

I could never claim to know everything about gypsies and I'm not a spokesperson for travellers. It's just that, like most people, I am fascinated by their world, and I really do feel lucky that I've been welcomed in by many of my customers as a friend. Not least because travellers' tales are always packed full of drama, high emotion and laughs, and I'm part of their story now too.

And that brings me to another reason that I am so fond of the gypsies I know. About ten years ago I went through something that most of us fear – something that probably tops the list of things that you never, ever want to go through: I was sent to prison. And through it all, along with my friends and family, my gypsy customers supported me, and their support is something that I will never forget.

Of course, I know that some people will always judge me and my relationship with travellers – and they are free to do so

– but if my time in prison taught me anything, it was not to judge others. And maybe that's why I get along with the gypsies so well: I treat them the same way that I treat everyone else – simply taking them as I find them.

The past fifteen years that my gypsy customers have been coming to me to make their dresses have been some of the most interesting times of my life. And the fascinating stories that have grown from working with them have also provided the backdrop to my own life story, which I will be revealing in this book.

You see, like the gypsy girls, I also got married very young. I wanted the best wedding ever, the biggest cake, the most beautiful dress, and, most of all, to be happy ever after. Now we all know that, no matter how nice your life may turn out to be, happy ever after is just a dream, a fairytale. And no one knows that more than me. But then no one believes in fairytales more than a gypsy girl who is about to become a bride.

And, as the Gypsy Dressmaker, it's my job to make her fairytale come true.

1

The Tale of How It All Began

I think it was around October. It was definitely 1996. And I will never forget it was winter because Dave, my partner, would always arrive at my flat early, it was always pitch black, and it was always *bloody* freezing. But I suppose we got used to it as every week was the same – we'd be out loading the van at five a.m., as careful as we could with the little ivory and white christening gowns and boys' suits that were beginning to make my stall one of the most talked-about on Paddy's Market.

Great Homer Street Market – to give it its real name – was the scruffiest-looking place you've ever seen. It's an Everton institution and it's been there forever. My mum's aunty even had a stall at Paddy's in the 1930s – that's how old it is. It's massive and it's got hundreds of indoor and outdoor stalls.

Now, I'll bet you every kid in Liverpool has been to Paddy's on a Saturday morning with their mum at some point, dragged around, feet sticking to the floor. There was always talk that Liverpool Council was going to redevelop Paddy's, and the indoor part was moved to a better spot over the road, but really, it hasn't changed, and I have always loved it. The stalls at Paddy's stretch right out and along Great Homer Street, so you'd always find all sorts there, from fruit stands to second-hand clothes stalls and furniture places or people selling off job lots, that kind of thing. Years ago you'd get moneylenders hanging about too. 'Mary Ellens' – that's what we used to call them.

When I set up my stall there the indoor part of the market was mainly filled with second-hand traders. Then, as you moved through, there would be other types of stalls – people who made their own stuff, like ladies' clothes, knitted clothes, curtains, jewellery and kids' clothes. Some of them were kind of homespun-looking, but some of it was really well made. The ones that always made me laugh, though, were the shoe stalls where they had big holes in the sides to pull string through so as to bind them together in a 'pair'. Even funnier was that people actually bought them.

So this was Paddy's, and every Saturday I'd set up my stall with children's clothes I'd designed and made myself. I'd sold there before, but this time my stall was bigger. It was in the indoor part of the market, in the middle aisle at the back, alongside the dressmakers and second-hand clothes traders.

It was mainly christening dresses I was doing then, but I'd make other accessories to go with them to make a set. There would be these tiny top hats and bibs with children's names embroidered on them. I'd even do these little ballet shoes. And bonnets – I loved making bonnets. I had had a thing about them ever since I was a kid and used to watch films like *Little Women*.

I taught myself how to make bonnets – no pattern; nothing. But I wanted to do them properly so I went to the library and looked for as many books about the American Civil War as I could find. I'd take them home and really study the pictures of the women in stiff peaked hats, you know, those ones with big ribbon ties under the chin.

I wanted to make my bonnets look exactly like the ones I saw in the books, and that meant making sure that I got every detail right, like the little frills inside the peaks. I would use different silks to create these, and it made all the difference. Then I'd add other details, like a huge bow on the side, say. The more I looked at the pictures of the bonnets in the books while I was making them, the more they turned out just like the ones I saw in films. They were lovely, they were, really lovely, and I'm sure that's what started selling the christening robes – everyone wanted the matching bonnets.

Dave had helped me make my stall look really nice. He said you couldn't see the little dresses very well when they were just hanging up, and that the way I had displayed them didn't do them justice.

Dave is a builder and is really good at making things, so it was his idea to do stands to put the dresses on. They really made a difference and the stall looked classy, which was an achievement because the market was a right mess and it wasn't unusual to see rats running around the back of the stalls. But after Dave did our corner up, it stood out. It took us two hours every Saturday morning to set up that stall. But it looked special – just rows and rows of pretty little white and ivory silk and satin dresses. It was quite talked about and people used to come by just to see it. Then the local press did a story on our stall and after that I got loads of interest, with people coming from miles around just to take photographs of the children's outfits. The business really started to take off then.

There were a lot of gypsies who used to come to the market – all the travellers go to Paddy's – but I didn't realise they were gypsies then. The one person I knew with connections to that world was a woman in the market known as Gypsy Rose Lee, whose stall was next to mine.

Now, Gypsy Rose is a Romany. But back then I didn't know the difference between a Romany and an Irish traveller, or whatever. I didn't even relate her to being a traveller. To us, she was just someone who read palms, like those women in Blackpool near the pier – the ones who stop you and say, 'Can I read your palm, love?'

Gypsy Rose was lovely. She was a good-looking woman with long, brown hair. She was kind and good company and not at all like the gypsies we were scared of as kids and that my mum had warned me about. I'll never forget seeing my mum hiding in the house one day when I was little. This woman had knocked on the door trying to sell lucky heather and pegs.

'Don't ever open the door to them,' Mum whispered, 'because if you don't buy off them they'll put a curse on you. And don't look one in the eye, right, or they'll put a curse on you. And if you ever meet one and they try to give you lucky charms, take them, because if you don't they'll put a curse on you for that too.'

I was terrified of gypsies after that. Since then, I've had loads of curses put on me. Honestly, loads of them.

But I do remember the first time I encountered a real gypsy. This girl came to see me at my stall and was looking at the christening dresses. Up she walked. Dead tall, she was. And blonde. Really stunning. She was about nineteen and I remember her because she was really friendly, a naturally nice girl, you know. Michelle, that was her name. I'll never forget her face. And I'll never forget Michelle's kids – gorgeous, they were. They stood out, all really blonde with pretty ringlets.

That's another reason I could sense something different about her – her kids just looked like they came from another era, as though they had stepped out of the pages of an old-fashioned story book.

'Can you do *Gone With the Wind* dresses?' she asked in a quiet voice.

You know by now what that film meant to me – *Gone With the Wind*, Scarlett O'Hara, velvet, big skirt, bonnet …

'Yeah,' I said, 'I can do that.'

'Well, how much will they be?'

I told her that I couldn't give her a price because I didn't use that kind of velvet at the time and I'd have to find out how much it cost.

'Well, I want three red ones,' she said, looking down at these three beautiful little girls trailing behind her.

'You'll have to leave a deposit,' I said.

She handed over £80 and I measured up the kids. She said she'd be back the next Saturday to pick them up.

So off I went, thinking about *Gone With the Wind* and all those big, hooped dresses. The moment in the film that made the biggest impression on me was when Scarlett O'Hara has no money and she pulls the curtains down so that she can use the fabric to make a dress. And the sound of the dresses! Oh, I loved the way you could hear the taffeta swish when Scarlett walked in the room. I adored these dresses. I remember watching it one time, thinking, 'Why don't we all dress like that?'

You know, in big dresses with tiny little waists and with beautiful bonnets on the side of our heads.

Could I do *Gone With the Wind* dresses? I don't think that girl could ever have known just how much she'd come to the right person. I couldn't wait to get stuck in and start making them.

I've still got pictures of these little red velvet dresses somewhere. They stuck right out, and had wide ribbon belts around the waist with big red bonnets to match. It nearly killed me making them, as I was trying to get them done in time for the girl coming back while having to make new stuff for the market on Saturday as well.

In the end I did finish them in time, and I'll always remember the struggle I had loading them into the van and carrying them to the market because the hooped underskirts weighed a ton. When I got to Paddy's I laid them flat, behind the stall, ready for this girl to come in and pick them up that morning, which was when she said she'd come back.

It was getting later and later, and so at about twelve o'clock I thought, 'These are going to get filthy lying through the back here by that dirty floor.' You only have so much space behind your stall at Paddy's, and people are always traipsing in and out, bringing more rubbish in with them. Not only that, there was a leak in the roof right above my area, so I thought, 'I'll just put them up with the other dresses for now.'

Baby Mary had just bought me a cup of tea. Her stall was right opposite mine. Baby Mary sold baby clothes and beautiful hand-knitted coats and hats. We were standing having a chat and she was looking up at the little *Gone With the Wind* dresses. 'They're lovely, them, aren't they?' she said. 'Just gorgeous.' I had to admit that they did look really nice. Another woman went by and said, 'God, they're lovely. How much are they?' I told her that they were actually sold and that the girl who ordered them was coming back to pick them up later.

Then I remembered that I had the girl's phone number, so I tried calling her. There was no answer; the phone didn't seem to work. Later, I would come to realise that this was normal with travellers – phones that don't work; numbers that don't exist; calls that are never returned.

It was the afternoon by now and I was still hoping she might turn up. I was standing there having another cup of tea when another girl walked past.

'How much are they, love?' she asked.

'About eighty quid,' I said, just picking the first price that came into my head, while also kind of knowing that was far too cheap because there was quite a lot of velvet in them.

Anyway, as the afternoon went on more and more people stopped to look at the little red dresses, with their little matching bonnets perched to the side.

'My God, there's a lot of interest in them, isn't there?' said Baby Mary.

'Yeah,' I thought. 'Isn't there just.'

At that point another woman walked by, then came back to take a closer look.

'Can you do them in different colours?' she asked.

It seemed that about every ten minutes people walking past were stopping to ask about the outfits. How much are these? Can you do them in this? Can you do them in that? How long will it take you to do them?

I was beginning to realise that something strange was happening. 'Who are these people?' I thought. 'Why are they so interested in these dresses?'

The thing is, when it first started to dawn on me that the young girl with the pretty kids wasn't going to come back and pick up the dresses, I was annoyed. 'If she doesn't buy these outfits, who the hell else is going to?' I wondered. They were just so over the top, all lace and frills and stuff, and I didn't much fancy the idea of carrying them back home again.

But then this stream of interested onlookers kept on. Some even went off and brought others back with them to have a look. By about quarter to three in the afternoon loads of people had stopped by my stall. 'What's going on here?' I wondered.

I noticed that the women who were stopping by were all rather similar, but different from the Liverpool girls who usually came to buy the christening stuff. They were all crowding around and getting quite close to me, as though they had no sense of personal space. It was pretty overpowering and really quite scary. I couldn't quite put my finger on what it was about them that really struck me most but, looking back, I guess it was the way that they spoke.

All gypsies speak differently – the Romanies and the English gypsies probably sound nearest to the way settled people speak but their accents are different still, so you know that they are not what they call country folk. But it was the Irish travellers who really made me sit up and take notice that something was going on: they speak so fast that they're hard to understand and they sound as though they're talking in a foreign language. They are very, *very* loud and they all speak over each other. I found it quite intimidating, so that day I just stood there looking and listening and wondering what the hell was going on.

I also remember that these women looked different to our usual customers. It wasn't instantly obvious, but I did notice that they were quite young, from the very young-looking – 14 or 15, say – to women in their late 20s and early 30s. And the young girls looked quite glitzy – in some cases a bit too racy, I remember. What with their tiny belly tops and short skirts, I thought that they were dressed quite inappropriately for their seemingly young years. Then the older women looked like they may have been big sisters – a bit more dressed-down and casual – but they talked to the younger girls as though they were their mums. All of them looked as though they cared about the way they looked, though, and I could tell that they had spent time doing their hair and things.

Their hair – that's another thing that struck me. Almost every one of these girls and young women had beautiful hair – long, glossy, tumbling blonde or jet-black flowing hair. They were all striking looking. And boy, did they make a noise.

'They're travellers,' said Gypsy Rose Lee.

I looked at her and then looked at all the girls crowding around the stall, and the penny started to drop. I was really fascinated then.

I took ten orders for those dresses that Saturday. After that first one, which I knew I'd undersold, I started asking for £100 per dress, as I needed more money for a roll of velvet in a different colour. It was getting nearer Christmas time, so a lot of them wanted red velvet, which was good because it meant that I could use up the 50-metre roll I had at home. As well as phone numbers, I took deposits from them all.

The next week I took a different style back with me, a more ornate dress with layers and layers of lace, a cape and what was to become my most sought-after top hat. I'd bought two rolls of velvet, as someone else wanted a dress in blue. I'd made it for the woman already, but as she wasn't coming in to pick it up for three weeks I put it on display on the stand. I got more orders that week than I'd ever had before.

I was still trying to make everything myself, but with all these new orders coming in that was becoming impossible. So

I asked a seamstress called Audrey, who I used to work with, to help me. Audrey had actually taught me to sew properly a few years back when I had my first children's clothes business, so she knew exactly what to do. Then we got another girl, Angela, and there were three of us doing it. We still had to work all week, with me working every night to get them done, though. The bonnets used to take the longest to do because Angela and Audrey found them tricky – maybe they hadn't watched *Gone With the Wind* as many times as I had. They gave it a good go, but their bonnets weren't quite as detailed as I knew they should be, so I had to do them myself, which was a nightmare as each one took about three hours to make. Finally, after lots of practice, I got the making time down to an hour.

By November I was getting loads more customers, so I thought I might start doing boys' outfits as well, as not many people were doing them. I started to make suits with little matching caps with feathers, or with a big, droopy tassel – like an emperor's hat. I also made old-fashioned Oliver Twist-style suits and caps. I got a reputation for doing boys' suits then. But I have to admit that these were no ordinary suits. Seeing pictures of them now reminds me of all those nights I stayed up to get them finished in time for the market. They were so over the top, but that's why I loved making them.

But then I've always loved historical costumes, especially the really old-fashioned ones that Henry VIII and Elizabeth I wore. All those big Tudor sleeves, lace collars and ruffs and things fascinated me. And anything Victorian – I just love Victorian styles.

One of my favourite things about the whole dressmaking process is going to the library to look at all the books about history and the clothes people wore in the old days. I liked the way the Little Princes in the Tower were dressed. You know, those two little boys who were locked up by their uncle hundreds of years ago. After looking at pictures of them I made these little gold, embroidered coats with little matching cravats for boys. They turned out really smart.

Of course, looking at all these old books gave me loads of new ideas, and the clothes I made were all very costume-like, I suppose, because that's what I liked. But I do remember feeling a bit worried that the boys' ones wouldn't sell because they were so different from what we had been doing.

As ever, though, Dave was quick to reassure me: 'You know what, babe, they're brilliant.' He said he'd never seen anything like them. Everyone knew Dave on the market then, because he used to come with me on Saturday mornings. He'd load all the stuff in his van and take me down there. But to give you an even better idea of the kind of man Dave really is – in the end he gave up his Everton season ticket to come and help me every Saturday.

Dave gave me confidence and encouraged me all the way. That felt good and it was great to have him around. Of course, he was right, I needn't have worried: the little boys' suits went down a storm.

I really loved doing Paddy's Market, and I became good friends with a lot of the other stallholders and regular customers there. We'd fetch each other cups of tea and look out for each other. We were like a family.

Occasionally, the DSS or the police used to come to Paddy's and do raids, looking for counterfeiters or people who were working while signing on. When someone heard that they were coming, word would spread through the market like a speeded-up Chinese whisper. You'd see people with dodgy DVDs and the like flying all over the place. The stalls would clear as if by magic. It was dead funny. We used to have some laughs on that market, we really did.

Just how much my Paddy's mates would look out for me would become clearer later when I was to go through what would be one of the worst times of my life. When the going got really rough, not only did my market friends not let me down, they stuck right by me.

Things did start to get a little strained, though, when the travellers came to my stall. They'd all crowd round at once – the sister, the mother, the kids – touching things, asking things, all trying to talk to me while I worked out a price for what they wanted. It was pandemonium.

Some of the travellers who didn't know I had a stall there, but who had seen other gypsies with the dresses, would come by and say things like, 'Oh God, I didn't know you were here. I've just given a deposit to the other woman around the corner for a dress, but I'm going to go round and get my money back.' And they would.

I think it got up the noses of some stallholders, who didn't seem that happy about the amount of attention I was getting. Some of them probably resented me for it. I suppose I can't really blame them, because at times my stall would be teeming with women placing orders.

'How much, love?' they'd ask – usually all at once, while talking to their kids and sisters at the same time, the kids talking over them.

'The price is on it, look, up there,' I'd say.

But then they'd start: 'Oh, go on, love, you can do better than that. I'm going to order three of them. I'll give you £1,000 now, love.'

Now, I hadn't seen £1,000 for a long time and so I'd be like, 'Oh, all right, go on then.'

The travellers always wanted discounts. But it wasn't just 10 per cent that they wanted off, and the same scene would be played out every time it came to the money bit. 'I haven't got any more money, love. Come on, that's all I've got, love. Oh, go on, love.'

Before I knew it I'd be making ten dresses, so though I'd just been given £1,000, I was already out of pocket. I was making those dresses for practically nothing.

I knew I'd have to change my tune, because if I didn't I was never going to make a profit. As it turned out I didn't have to think about it too much, as it just happened quite naturally one Saturday. We were really busy and the stall was chaos – all these women chattering and shouting out all over the place. I thought my head was going to burst open. Only my mouth did instead.

'*That's it!*' I screamed. 'Nobody is getting served until you all *shut up!*'

'Oh, love. Sorry, love,' said one of the women. 'We don't mean any harm. We just talk loud. It's just our way.'

They weren't so perturbed and I realised that she was right, that was just their way, and if I wanted these women to carry on buying my dresses I'd just have to find my way of dealing with their way. From then on I got into the bargaining and even started to enjoy it. All I had to do, I learned, was stick to my guns. And it all added to the chaotic nature of the market.

Whether it was the travellers, local Liverpool girls, or the occasional raids, there was never a dull moment at Paddy's, because if there's one thing that flea markets throughout the world have in common, it's great characters. And my stall was surrounded by them.

There was Baby Mary opposite me, Second-hand Mary over on one side, and Dancing Mary, who used to do all the dancing gear for kids at the back of me, and a regular at the market, Mary Hughes. Honest to God, I think they were all Marys!

Then there was Second-hand Joan. She was a real con merchant. Second-hand Joan used to borrow money from everyone but always seemed to have trouble paying it back. Second-hand Mary and Baby Mary had warned me never to lend Second-hand Joan anything.

Funnily enough, about three years ago Joan came into Nico, my shop in Liverpool that you might have seen me in when *Big Fat Gypsy Weddings* was on TV. She asked me if I had any old stuff that I could give her for her stall. I was happy to offload bits and bobs that we had lying around, so I went off upstairs to have a look. Joan followed me, but when we got up there I turned around and she literally fell to her knees.

'Please help me, Thelma,' she cried. 'Help me. Please help me! I've got to pay all this money.' She asked me to lend her £2,000. I just looked at her. It was all a bit awkward.

'I just don't have that kind of money to give you right now, Joan,' I said.

'Oh, but can you get me it? Can you get me it?' she sobbed.

I felt sorry for her, as I knew that feeling. 'Yeah,' I said, 'I'll try. But for God's sake, get up, Joan!'

I quickly walked back downstairs. Pauline – who has been my trusty right-hand woman for as long as anyone can remember, but who no one forgets – was staring at me as we walked down. She had a look on her face that said: 'Don't you dare – don't you *dare* trust her.' We managed to calm Joan down a bit and got her to leave.

Then, just as if someone had written it in a play, who should walk in minutes later but Baby Mary. It was like Paddy's Market days all over again. 'Give her nothing,' she said. 'She owes so and so and so and so. She's borrowed some money from some woman on the market and her husband has come down and said, "You get my wife's money back now!" So now she's come to you to get it.'

I didn't give Joan the money – though I did think about it, because, as you'll find out, it wasn't that many years before that I had been in a desperate situation myself. I felt genuinely sorry for her. And I had been pleased to see her again because I used to talk to her a lot on the market.

But that night I went to the bingo with my mum and who should be sitting there playing? Joan! Yes, the woman with no money – out playing bingo! But then, you'll always get her type on a market.

After a few months at Paddy's, I'd kind of started to recognise the travellers from the other people at the market. One day this woman came to the stall – older than most of the traveller girls that came in – and I wasn't sure if she was a traveller or not. She told me she had nine sons and had just had a baby girl after twenty years. She was absolutely besotted with the child.

This woman was from London, and had heard about me and our dresses, so she'd made the trip up to Liverpool with her husband to find me. That Saturday will always stick in my mind because when her husband came over he looked around the outfits on the stall and, after about four seconds, looked at me and said, 'I'll take the lot.'

And he did. He took every single thing I had that day that would fit the little girl. Everything. And just before they turned to leave he said, 'I want you to make more for her because we live in London and we're going back there. Can you make me all different ones? In different colours?' I think I worked solidly for three weeks after that, just making dresses for that woman's baby.

I knew that the dresses we made were special, and as the travellers used to request that more and more be added to the designs they started to look even more so. But sometimes I remember thinking while I was making them, 'How the hell are the poor kids going to walk in these?' I suppose, as some of them were for girls who were only around six months old, that wouldn't be such a problem. But they were big and heavy and they really stuck out. And sometimes the little ruff necks would be stiff because I couldn't use anything softer to make them stand up. So I'd suggest to the women that it might be a good idea to have a different design and to maybe leave out the hoop so that the baby could move a little easier.

'I don't think this will be very comfortable, you know, for the baby to lie in,' I'd say.

'No, no, love, she'll be all right, she'll be all right,' they'd come back. These women were determined to have the biggest and best, regardless.

Not so long ago I was reminded of those days when I had gone to meet some English gypsies at their house, which was a massive place in Morecambe. I was a little bit apprehensive about going at first, as the travellers can be a bit wary of you if they don't know you, and some of the Romany and English gypsies were not happy at the way they had been portrayed on the TV programme. So I was thinking, 'Oh, we're going to get a right reception here.'

But when we walked in they were all just so happy to see me. Pauline and me got chatting to them and one of the young girls came up to me and said: 'I've got a dress you made for me when I was four. Do you remember?' I couldn't, because she must have been about sixteen or seventeen by this time. 'Have you still got it?' I asked. So she ran upstairs and brought down this little brown and ivory velvet dress.

At that point her dad walked in and said, 'Do you remember we came to your house on Christmas Eve to pick it up?'

'God,' I said. 'Yeah, I do remember that!' It was about thirteen years ago. 'Bloody hell,' I thought, looking at that dress again. It was still in perfect condition, still in its bag and everything. It was short and sticky-out, made in velvet panels that were all braided around the edge, and it had a little coat that went over it, with a tiny muff and a beret. I had seen that outfit on a woman in a book about the 1800s and then made my own little version of it.

When I looked at that dress it brought back all these really happy memories of that time at Paddy's in the late 1990s and how everything had started to pick up with those little *Gone With the Wind* dresses. They really were sweet.

I suppose my original Victorian designs look a bit dated now, when you think about the requests we get for Communion dresses these days, with their giant skirts, hundreds of ruffles, miles of material and all the glittery crystals and crowns, and the kids turning up to church in their own pink limos. And I couldn't be happier doing all the fantastic and elaborate designs that we are asked for today, but I do have fond memories of making these early designs, of being so determined to get them right, so that all these gorgeous little kids would look like characters out of a film, all perfectly pretty. And I'm dead chuffed when my long-standing traveller customers want to pull them out and show me those early ones again. Luckily, my English and Romany customers still like to dress their kids in these romantic old styles, so I do still get a chance to make them.

By the end of that first year on the market I'd got to know a little bit more about the travellers' ways; I suppose I'd started to accept their way of doing things and was becoming less surprised that travellers' lives weren't much like mine. But a memory that still really sticks in my mind was of a little girl hanging about the stall in December. She was looking at the dresses while her mum was settling up for orders and she was chattering away about how they were all going to meet on Christmas Day and Boxing Day. Then she said something about them all being in their trailers. It had never actually occurred to me that gypsies still lived in caravans.

'Bloody hell,' I thought, 'how are you all going to get round the Christmas table in a caravan with these dresses on?' I thought of all these lovely little girls in all their lovely little velvet dresses ... Then I pictured all of them covered in chocolate on Christmas Day. I didn't feel as romantic about the whole thing after that.

But then I was exhausted. It had been a rollercoaster couple of months and I knew I needed a rest before our busiest time of the year – First Communion season, which was going to start as soon as Christmas and New Year were over.

'Thank God it's Christmas Eve,' I said to Dave, when he got back from delivering our last order to a traveller site in Leeds. 'At least they're not going to want any of these dresses in summer ...'

2

The Tale of the First Communion Dresses

My gypsy customers started coming back to Paddy's the first few weeks in January. Only now they were coming from all over the country, not just Liverpool or Manchester but from London and Ireland too. As I was getting to know them all a little better, I started giving my phone number out to some of the travellers. They had also started to talk to me more.

One Saturday, a girl approached the stall with a pram. She had a big black coat on and was wrapping it tightly around her. The coat seemed huge because she was tiny. She was very, very young, and, to be honest, looked like she had the world on her shoulders. She kind of shuffled up.

'Are you the Liverpool woman who makes the dresses?' she asked, softly. 'I want dresses made for two little girls,' she said, pointing to the pram.

I looked down and saw these two tiny little things. One looked around twelve months old, the other a newborn baby. 'I want them really sticking out.' And then I want this, and I want that, the young girl carried on. She said that she wanted a bonnet for the really tiny one, who I noticed, when I looked in at her properly, was so small that she looked premature.

'I'm not sure that the dresses are quite right for your newborn,' I said to her.

'Oh, she's not newborn, she's ten months. And she's two,' she said, pointing at the older baby. They really were the smallest babies I've ever seen.

Then the girl started asking if she could have diamonds on the dresses. Now, she was the first traveller to ask for diamonds, and as I'd never done that before I was a bit unsure. So I told her, 'I can't start them without half the money as a deposit.' She said she'd go and get the money and be straight back. So off she went.

Ever since the stall had become popular with the travellers, a lot of the other stallholders had been warning me against working with them. 'Be careful. Don't trust them. Just don't trust them,' they'd say.

Surprisingly, Gypsy Rose Lee was always stressing the point. But by then I realised that she was different from them. Gypsy Rose was Romany. Romanies are wary of other travellers and, to be honest, sometimes I think they see themselves as a cut or two above them.

Gypsy Rose's kids were around her stall all the time. They were lovely, really well-behaved, and they'd go and get us all cups of tea. The other traveller kids that came to us, on the other hand, mostly Irish, were loud and boisterous and just so full of confidence. And the language! My God, it was terrible. But I soon got used to that and realised it's just the way they speak. It's not threatening or anything.

So, I waited for the girl who wanted the diamond dresses to come back, and deep down I suppose I never expected to see her again – the travellers are always full of promises of coming back but quite often they don't. But she did, and this time she had her husband in tow. He was carrying one of the babies and was smothering her in kisses. 'What a lovely dad,' I thought, surprised at how kind and affectionate he was being. He looked up at me and said, 'How much are the dresses going to be?'

Now, for the tiny little baby's outfit the girl had said that she wanted a diamond collar and diamond cuffs. She wanted diamanté all over the dresses, basically. I didn't know a trade supplier of Swarovski crystals, so I knew I'd have to buy them at the full retail price, which would be dear.

'£600 for the two,' I said, thinking he'd say 'No way', saving me all the trouble of having to make such a tricky order.

But he didn't even think about it. He put his hand in his pocket, flicked through the notes and handed me the cash. As they left I remember standing there thinking: 'Jesus, I'd better make sure these dresses are *really* nice.' The couple came back a few weeks later to pick them up. The young mum was over the moon.

A month or so after that I was talking to another traveller woman, Mary – Mary Connors. She was a good-looking woman, Mary, tall with long, brown, wavy hair. You could tell, just by looking at her, that she must have been stunning as a girl. By the time I got to know Mary she must have been around 35 and had had seven kids. She still had a cracking figure, though, and I always liked the way she dressed. Mary was smart and classy looking and would wear long skirts with boots, that kind of thing. She had a neat style, well-off looking, you know?

The other thing I liked about Mary was her confidence. She had an air of authority about her and I knew that she was well liked in the community. The fact that she had seven children earned her the respect of her peers, as the more children a traveller woman has the more status she gets. I always liked seeing Mary with her kids – she was a really warm person and a good mum. Her kids adored her.

But Mary was tough, and even though she was only in her mid-30s, you could tell that she had lots of experience. She was wise and taught me a lot, and would come to the stall just for a chat, asking how things were going and whether I'd had more traveller customers. When I described to her who had come in, she instantly knew who the family was and would tell me all about them. In a way Mary was educating me, teaching me more and more about the travellers that would finally make my business.

So she'd become a bit of a regular on the stall, and though we didn't know each other really well then, we hit it off and she obviously enjoyed my company as much as I did hers, so she was always popping in for a gossip. One day she came in and asked me: 'Did you do Margaret's dresses for the wedding?'

'Who's Margaret?' I said.

'Margaret, you know, Sweepy's Margaret?'

The thing is, the gypsies think that you know everyone that they do because they live in such a closed community and all know each other. But I had no idea who Margaret was. Also, in my experience all traveller women seemed to be called Margaret or Mary!

'Oh, they were handsome, love,' she said. 'All these diamonds on them. Oh, they were really handsome.'

Then, of course, I knew who she was talking about.

'Do you know him, love?' she asked, meaning the man who'd given me the cash that day.

'No, not really,' I told her.

'Oh, he's a multi-millionaire,' said Mary. I was gobsmacked, thinking back to the day that I first set eyes on young Margaret, remembering that black coat and how she was the poorest-looking soul I'd ever seen.

I know the family really well now. The girls in that pram are all grown up and they love the fact that they were the first to get their dresses covered in diamonds. They still talk about it.

Shannon, the two-year-old, is 16 now, and the really tiny one that I was worried about, Shamelia, is 15. They've got two more sisters now as well, and we have made swishy little dresses for them since they were little too. Shannon and Shamelia are a great barometer of how traveller tastes have changed. When we first started making designs for them their mum wanted all the Victorian stuff, but with lots of glitter, really pretty dresses. Now that the girls are older and have their own ideas about how they want to dress, it's all sparkly Swarovski-covered catsuits and the like. They've grown up to be really gorgeous, lovely kids, these girls.

The thing is, travellers always like to dress their children well. And, you know, I think Liverpool people are exactly the same as gypsies that way, because if you don't have much to call your own, your whole pride comes from how good your kid looks. Nothing feels better than to have your child with you, dressed up so nice that people stop and say, 'Oh, look at what she's wearing.' You just want to give your kids everything. There are probably more designer kids' boutiques in Liverpool than anywhere else today. Yet for the Liverpool mum there are never, ever enough.

I'm the same myself. About thirty years ago I bought my daughter Hayley a pair of shoes that cost around £70. To be honest, she wasn't even at the walking stage, but I didn't care, I just loved dressing my kids up.

A few years back, when my youngest daughter, Katrina, who's seven now, went to nursery, all the girls who worked there used to get so excited when I dropped her off. I wasn't on the telly then, so they didn't know I was a dressmaker. 'We can't wait to see what she's got on when she comes in,' they'd say. So I thought, 'Oh, I'll definitely need to make sure I have something new on her every day if they are waiting to see what she's wearing!' Now I'm the same with my granddaughter Phoebe – I buy her new outfits all the time.

It's such a Liverpool thing – maybe you need to come from Liverpool to understand it. You see, when I was a kid, no matter how little money we had, I always had the best dress and, from as far back as I can remember, I knew exactly what I wanted to wear: dream-come-true dresses that moved when you moved, dresses where you could feel the weight of the fabric swinging about you as you walked.

Once my mum asked this woman, who used to make costumes for the dancing school I went to, if she would make me a couple of day dresses. I was so excited when we went to collect them. The first one was pink with lots of frothy net under it and a big tie belt wrapped into a big bow at the side. As soon as I put that one on, I just didn't want to take it off. I had to, though, because I had to try on the other one.

Now, this other one was probably a lovely dress but it was straight up and down with a pleated hem. As soon as I saw it I thought, 'No! No! No!' I looked at my mum and started crying. She told me to try it on. 'I don't want it,' I wailed. 'Get it off me!'

'No, no, they're lovely,' my mum said to the woman as she paid for the dresses, obviously dead embarrassed, trying to rush me out the door. So off we went back home with both of the dresses. But I never did wear that straight dress. I never wanted it. All I ever wanted were pretty, girly, sticky-out dresses. So when these young gypsy girls come to me now, I know exactly why they want them too. But then I've always had a strong vision in my head of what the perfect girl's dress should be.

Back in the early eighties, long before I'd set up at Paddy's, I'd just had my youngest daughter Hayley. On Saturdays I used to go shopping with my mum, and we'd go to all the little kids' boutiques in Liverpool looking for clothes for her.

The thing is, I could never find anything that I really liked and I remember thinking I'd like to do kids' clothes myself. I'd just had a baby and was looking at it from the point of view of what I'd like to dress her in, as a customer. 'If I can't find the right thing,' I thought, 'then there must be loads of other mums out there who feel the same.'

More than anything else, though, I just wanted to dress Hayley the way I liked. I thought about it a lot, and then it just came to me: I'll start up my own children's clothes business. And so I went about setting up a shop, Madine Miniatures. At the time I was married to Kenny, my three older kids' dad. Kenny already had a successful glass firm, so we were well-off enough for me to give it a go. And things were not that great with me and Kenny by then, so starting the business was also a good way of taking my mind off our troubles at home. My mum had also just been made redundant from the GEC factory, where she had worked as one of her three jobs for twenty-five years. So she put all her redundancy money in to get the business started.

Soon it was up and running and I threw myself into the task of finding out when all the clothing fairs were on. I'd travel the country with my mum, looking for the best stuff we could find.

The first shop I opened was in Ormskirk, just north of Liverpool. But as there was already a kids' clothing boutique there the reps would give them priority stock and wouldn't sell to any competitors. But this meant that I was being left with the not-very-good stuff, which I certainly didn't want. What I wanted to sell were special children's outfits, the kind that gave me butterflies in my stomach when I looked at them.

I remember talking to one rep and asking if I could order this particular dress. 'Sorry, you can't have that,' he said, in that nose-in-the-air kind of way, explaining that so-and-so from the other shop had bought it. I looked at him and thought, 'You cheeky get! One of these days, you'll be dying for me to stock your clothes!'

'Don't worry, love,' my mum used to say, 'you'll think of something. We'll just make sure you're the biggest and the best.' The thing is, the man was the rep for all these lovely Italian, German and Dutch designs that you couldn't get over here. 'OK,' I thought, 'I'll just go to Italy, Germany and Holland to buy this stuff myself.' And that's exactly what I did – I brought ranges of kids' clothing to Liverpool that nobody had ever seen or even heard of before.

I had a big opening day for that first shop, and everything felt good. Because we'd made sure that Madine Miniatures was stocked with quite unusual kids' clothes and unique designs, it really took off, and before long we had six shops all over Liverpool. Madine Miniatures was getting a great reputation and our Communion dresses were the most sought-after in the city.

Communion dresses are a very big deal in Liverpool, with it being such a big Catholic community. Even today a big part of my business is designing Communion dresses. And there are three milestones in a gypsy girl's life – her christening, her First Communion and, of course, her wedding.

I first started doing Communion dresses after noticing that all the ones I'd see at European suppliers were the same. And the one thing that a mum doesn't want is her daughter's Communion dress looking the same as the next girl's. I'd look at them and think: 'They're all straight up and down. They don't move. Where's all the bloody fabric?' And then I thought: 'I'd make the skirt bigger and I wouldn't have that there; I would put buttons down here ...' I was not very impressed by what I was looking at – but actually what I was really looking at was a giant gap in the market.

So I decided that the best thing to do was to make the dresses myself. Even though I couldn't sew that well, I knew exactly what I wanted. My mum had learned how to sew at a night class when me and my brother Tom were kids. She would sit up all night making me new dresses, determined that I would always be the best-dressed little girl at school. Also, my Aunty Mary was a tailoress, so I thought, 'I have all the ideas in my head, all I have to do is to draw them out and Mum and Aunty Mary can make them.' I used to watch my mum and Aunty Mary sewing and then have a go myself. I wasn't very good at it at first, but I wouldn't give up until I got it perfect.

Soon the dresses were going down really well. Everyone wanted them, and after a while we were getting so many orders that we had to think about getting someone else in to help. Thank God we found Audrey. Now, Audrey was a little bit older but that was good because she was old school. She knew exactly what she was doing.

In fact, Audrey was so by the book that, come five p.m. every day, she'd have her coat on and she'd be off. Out the door by one second past, was Audrey. She was strictly a nine-to-fiver, but I have to give it to her, when she was there she didn't stop for a minute. But as more orders came in we needed to put more time in, which made me determined to improve as a seamstress. Audrey taught me a lot – far more than the college I had started attending did. The more I learned, the more I could finish the dresses myself. We also took on a younger girl, Christine, to do the cutting. So, business was picking up, we were all working from a room above the shop in Ormskirk and everything was good.

Every time we put a new Communion dress in the shop, people would come in and admire it. 'Oh, isn't that lovely,' they'd say. 'I'm quite good at this,' I thought, so I just focused on making my ideas for these Communion dresses come to life. I suppose, looking back, I've always been the kind of person who sets her mind to things, thinking, 'Right, I'm just going to do it.' I can't do anything half-heartedly.

After I came up with a few dress design ideas, I started really going for it. I always thought that the dresses could be bigger, because no one else was doing ones like that, so I looked through all my history books and wedding magazines for ideas – because, essentially, they were little wedding dresses. I'd have them with these big, Victorian-style leg-o'-mutton sleeves and then maybe add a little cape. And I always liked to put a large bow or flower on them to finish them off. That way they really made a statement.

People loved them and, as more and more requests came in for them, we started having to limit each school to ten differently designed Communion dresses. The way it worked was this: every season I'd create ten different designs, and the first mum from each school to put a deposit down on the design she liked best was the only one who could have that dress, and so on. It meant that ten little girls in the same school might be wearing our dresses come Communion Day, but there would never be two wearing the same one.

Even so, there was often pandemonium over who got these dresses, with real rivalry breaking out between the mums at each school. I remember that there were women literally fighting in the shop in County Road. Honest to God, they were actually punching each other.

Another time I did this dress – I think I was into Elizabeth I at the time – with the ruff collar and the really tight, tiny waist with a V-shaped bodice all covered in pearls. I made the skirt in satin panels, which were differently decorated. Everyone who saw it was like, 'Oh My God, it's amazing. It's fantastic. I don't care how much it is. I've got to have that dress.' There was a big hullabaloo over who was going to get that too.

The thing is, it was all good for business and I was able to start building up a team. I took on another three girls, and then Pauline started working in the County Road shop. Pauline had been a customer originally, but as time went on she began to pop in every day to have a chat and see the new dresses that had come in. She became such a part of the furniture that one day, when I was run off my feet, I asked her to muck in and help me out there and then. I was well aware that Pauline knew that shop – and the stock it carried – inside out.

It was one of the best moves I ever made. Pauline is the best saleswoman you could ever wish for. We have worked together on and off ever since. Pauline whipped our customers up into a right frenzy about the Communion dresses. 'Oh, you should see the new designs coming in,' she'd say. 'They're gorgeous. You'll be amazed when you see them.' All the women, desperate that their kid would look the best of the lot, would be like, 'Oh, put my name down for one, put my name down.' None of these dresses ever reached the shop – because before they could get there Pauline had sold every single one.

So, it was really through the Communion dresses that I first got into dressmaking. And all these things that I liked, all these old, historical costumes that I was influenced by, were obviously touching a nerve with people, because the next thing I knew I had an agent in Belfast who started selling our dresses all over Ireland.

The business was doing well and everything was OK on that front. But things with me and Kenny were getting worse. The more successful I became, the more strained things were between us. Kenny, you see, always liked to be in control, and as I became immersed in my own thing I was becoming more independent.

Then I had another setback. The main shop in Liverpool kept getting broken into, and this put a massive strain on the business because it was becoming increasingly hard to get insurance. Eventually the only way I could keep things afloat was to close all of the shops except two. Looking back, it was probably too much having six of them and trying to make clothes and sell them at the same time.

There had also been a dispute over outstanding rent at the Ormskirk shop that we had sub-let. The woman who took it on refused to pay the rent because of a repair that had not been done. She moved out and left us with the bill. So, in what would be the first of many court appearances over the coming years, I was made bankrupt. I was distraught. But when I got my head around it I realised that things weren't as bad as I had at first thought.

By this time Kenny had sold his business and he suggested that I put my business in his name, which of course meant that, effectively, I would be working for him. Businesswise it did seem to be the only way forward. We had a big house with loads of land, and a big garage too, so I was able to bring all the girls to work there, and that meant we could cut down on overheads.

The only difference was that when I had to go and buy fabric in Manchester Kenny would have to sign blank cheques for me to take, as he was in charge of the business bank account. Eventually it became impossible for me to have all the cheques I needed every time I wanted to buy something, so I would just sign them in his name. I thought he was fine with that – it wasn't a big deal. Not then, anyway.

After the last robbery at the Liverpool shop, the police finally caught the thieves, so as part of the insurance claim I had to go to court to confirm that these people had no permission to be in my shop. As I was going up to the courtroom in the lift, two policemen and a young lad got in. I heard them talking and this lad – he must have been about 20 – looked at me and said: 'Was it your shop we robbed?'

'Yeah,' I said, looking at him, surprised.

'No offence, love, but you didn't half pile it on there, did you?' he said, trying to make out that our claim was higher than the shop stock was worth.

'It's all expensive designer stuff, you know,' I said, affronted.

'Ah well, nothing personal,' he smirked.

Then, as the lift stopped and the police started to usher him out, do you know what the cheeky little get did? He turned to me and asked: 'Sure you don't want any videos or owt?' Some people just can't help themselves, can they?

But it was around this time that everything started to really go wrong. Since Kenny had sold his business he wasn't working and so he was getting up at around midday and then going out and not coming back until early hours in the morning. I'd still be working in the garage, and he'd pop his head around the garage door and say, 'You still working?'

'Yes, I'm still working,' I would think to myself, looking at him. 'I'm the only one in this house working.' In fact I was working all hours to try and rebuild the business and to keep the family going, after he had sold his business. But the bank account was in his name. I was still bankrupt and now Kenny was in control.

Our marriage had been rocky for a while, and the children were growing up. Hayley, my youngest, was now 12, Tracey was 19, and my son Kenny was 20. He had moved into a flat with his girlfriend, and they had just had a baby, Daniel – my first grandchild.

So, after years of always being at home or working all hours, I started going out with Pauline on Friday nights. Pauline understood what I was going through with Kenny and tried to take my mind off things. She is a good singer and she liked to enter all the pub karaoke competitions. They were a really big deal in Liverpool pubs at the time and you could earn good money if you won.

I started going with her on Sundays too, and Kenny didn't like it. By this time, though, I didn't care that we didn't do anything together. Then I heard that he was seeing someone else. Had I been told that a few years back I would have been devastated, but I had started building a life of my own by then and I was enjoying my evenings out with Pauline. In the end, me and Kenny were just keeping up appearances, but because we had Hayley, who was still quite young, to think about, we kept going. I wanted her to be brought up by two parents, her mum and dad, like her brother and sister had been.

And, on the face of it, me and Kenny had the perfect marriage – big house, nice car, lovely kids. But he had let me down time and again. He just couldn't take the responsibility of looking after a family, and I was the one who was left to do that. But boy, did he make me suffer.

Still, we lived in a lovely house in a nice area. How could I take that away from my kids? The thought of it made me stay in my marriage far longer than I knew I should.

Then, one Friday night, Kenny came home and said he wanted to talk. He was all dead nice and said, 'Listen, I don't want to keep going out on my own, and I want you to stop doing that too.'

I looked at him and said, 'No, I don't want to stop. If you want to stop going out then that's up to you, but I'm not.' I knew then that there was nothing left between us. It was the end. I had spent so many years doing what he wanted and being frightened not to. Now it felt easy; I wasn't scared to say what *I* wanted.

The following Monday morning, me and Pauline and the other girls in the Central Station shop were all standing around talking and catching up on the weekend. No one was more surprised than me to see Kenny coming up to the shop. He opened the door and walked right up to me. 'My shop – give me the keys,' he barked.

His shop! Yes it was in his name, but it was my mum's money and my hard work that built up the business. Still, I picked them up, looked straight at him and said, 'Here you are.' Then I turned around and said, 'Come on, girls,' and we walked out of the shop.

Kenny just stood there, watching. Me and the girls, who were a little bit in shock, went around the corner to this little café. Then we phoned the Indian fella who owned the shop opposite ours and asked him to look across to see what Kenny was doing.

'Can you see anything?' we kept asking him. 'What's he doing now?' He said he could see loads of women coming into the shop. It was Communion time, so it was one of our busiest periods. We were all laughing at the thought of Kenny standing there with his hands open, not knowing what to do. But I just thought, 'You know what, let him have it.' And I did. He got the shop, but I felt free.

Just after that Kenny moved out and set up home with his girlfriend.

Apart from the kids, the business was his last hold over me. He couldn't do anything then. Nothing. The shop closed down pretty soon after. But I couldn't sleep for thinking about the customers who had come to us to have their Communion dresses made. I still had all the numbers and all the books, so

I chased up the girls who had left deposits and said, 'OK, no problem. I'll do your dress for you and deliver it when it's done.' But we hadn't managed to contact all the people, so I rang the local radio station and asked them if they could do a little appeal, asking the people I couldn't contact to get in touch with me. They read it out over the air, and it worked! I managed to finish every order. At night, I'd jump in the car with Pauline and go round delivering them all.

Kenny still came to the house, and each time he came he would take more and more away with him. One September night he came to the house, picked up my car keys and drove off in our car.

It was my car too – I had bought it with money I had earned – but it was in his name. The worst thing about that was that we lived in a place that was quite out of the way, so I really needed a car to get around and to ferry Hayley about to all her mates'.

I was really upset by that. I called Pauline to tell her that I wouldn't be able to come and see her sing in the karaoke final. But she wasn't having any of it. 'Get down here now,' she said. 'Don't sit there on your own, crying – that's just what he wants. Get a taxi and I'll pay for it when you get here.' She was right. I called the taxi.

That night Pauline introduced me to Ruth, a woman she had met at some of the singing competitions. Pauline had told Ruth what was happening with me and Kenny, and Ruth asked me more. I spent most of that evening pouring my heart out to her.

'What's your biggest problem?' she asked me, trying to get some perspective on the situation.

'Well, apart from the fact that I've no car, no business, no money, and am bankrupt, where do you want me to start?' I said to her, with tears starting to run down my face.

On top of that, I'd just received a healthy amount of orders from my agent in Ireland that morning. 'Now I'll have to call her and tell her that I can't do them,' I said to Ruth. To my amazement she offered to help.

'What do you need to fulfil the Irish orders?' she asked.

'About £5,000 for fabric and a car to go to the warehouses,' I told her.

'Come and see me tomorrow,' she said. I couldn't believe it. Here was a complete stranger offering to help me. I suppose alarm bells should have rung then, but I was probably the most vulnerable I'd ever been and I needed a lifeline. I needed someone to hold on to.

I went to Ruth's house and she told me her plans. Her boyfriend would lend me the money I needed, and she suggested that, rather than me carrying on by myself, she and I could go into business together. She told me she had a business degree, so if I made the dresses she could look after the financial side of things. She set up a bank account in the name of My Fair Lady and rang the agent in Ireland explaining that she would be dealing with the business while I got on with the dressmaking. She set up credit accounts with some of the suppliers too.

When she came to my house one night to drop off some fabric, her jaw dropped when she saw where I lived. 'I used to live in a house like this, about fifteen years ago,' she told me, her voice filled with regret. 'That's until my ex-husband kicked me and the kids out on Christmas Eve.' Ruth went on to tell me more about her past life. I felt for her – her story sounded so similar to mine.

The next day I made a start on the orders. That evening Ruth arrived at my door in floods of tears. Her boyfriend had run off with everything in the house, she told me, including my computer and other things I had lent her to get the business up and running.

I tried to calm her down. She said she would think about how to get the money and then she said, 'Have you got any jewellery that we could pawn? It will keep us going until we get the money together.' I had never been in a pawn shop in my life and didn't know what to do. 'Give it to me and I'll sort it out,' Ruth convinced me. In the meantime, in my desperation I turned to the only person I could and asked my Aunty Gladys to lend me £3,000 to keep things going.

We bought more fabric with the money and I carried on with the orders. 'We should open a stall on the market with the old stock from your garage,' Ruth suggested. So we did. She set up at Paddy's and started selling there on Saturdays. Things went well for a bit, but then trade started to slow down when the First Communion season came to an end. So Ruth found a unit in another retail space and I started to make christening outfits for her to sell in it. But I had started to feel a bit unsure of Ruth, as she was becoming over-friendly. Then Ruth and Pauline stopped getting on and Pauline stopped working with us.

All this time, Tracey and Hayley were still in the family home. But I had no money whatsoever, not a penny, and I had to keep working to supply the shop as I needed to keep the house going. I also wanted to pay my aunty back as soon as I could. It was tough. In fact, it was turning out to be the hardest winter I'd had.

It's funny how things work out, though, because me and my kids ended up having a cracking Christmas that year. When I was with Kenny, and used to consider leaving him, I would say to myself, 'What would you do at Christmas?' But we had a ball.

The house was massive and we didn't have any oil for heating, and it was freezing, so the only thing for it was to go to the pub – me, Hayley, Tracey and her boyfriend. I stuck a duck in the oven and we all went for a couple of drinks (though, of course, Hayley was only drinking Coke). By the time we got back from the pub the duck was burnt. But we ended up playing games and having such a good laugh together that it didn't matter. We had no money but we had a good time.

A couple of days into the new year I got a call from Audrey, the seamstress who had worked for me and taught me in the early days. She told me that Ruth had been in touch, asking if she and one of the other girls wanted to come and work for her, because I didn't want to do the dresses any more. Ruth was trying to cut me out. I went down to see her in the unit. I was livid. 'I want nothing more to do with you,' I screamed at her.

And then it just clicked: I was the business. Without my skills, my contacts and the generosity of my family, Ruth's 'business' would never have got off the ground. Had I not been at such a low point that night I met her in the pub, and had I looked at things calmly instead of getting in a panic about what was happening with Kenny, I could have done everything myself. It dawned on me then that all I had done was to replace a controlling husband with a controlling friend.

'I'm taking over the stall in Paddy's,' I told Ruth. 'You can keep everything else.'

3

The Tale of My First Big Fat Gypsy Wedding Dress

So that's how I came to be at Paddy's all these years ago. Now it was January 1997 and my trickle of travellers had turned into a stream.

One Saturday, one of my regular gypsy customers came up and pointed at a dress. 'I'm going to a wedding. Can you do this for her?' she asked, looking down at her little girl.

'Yeah,' I said, 'no problem,' and started measuring up.

'Can you do me one for the next wedding too? It's my brother's wedding next.'

'Bloody hell,' I said, looking up at her. 'There's a wedding every week in your family. How often do you go to weddings?'

'Oh, nearly every week,' she said. I just laughed.

The stall was getting more and more crowded, and Saturdays were becoming a bit intense. Some days it felt as though I'd done thousands of orders. I'd be measuring up one kid and then some other woman would say, 'Over here, love, will you do her one, love?' And I'd be like, 'Yeah, yeah,' trying to write the other measurements down.

'Measure here, love, measure here,' another voice would pipe up. Then I'd look and there would be four of them behind the counter, and a baby.

'Don't touch, don't touch,' I said, trying not to sound too tetchy. They were my customers at the end of the day, and I wanted to treat them well. But, honestly, it was chaos, with kids running over there, under here … There were travellers all over the place.

Then the queues started. I'd open up at nine a.m. and soon a line would start to form. I used to feel guilty about keeping people waiting, so I'd ask if they wanted a cup of tea and send out the Saturday girl. 'I'll just deal with this and I'll come back to you,' I'd say. 'Just give me a minute.'

Only it always took longer than I expected, because when it came to giving them the price for what they'd ordered the traveller women wanted to stand and haggle with me all day. Or I'd be in the middle of serving the next family, and the first family would come back and add to the order that we'd already agreed a price for.

'Can you just do me a red one as well, love, put a red one on that?' So, I'd be like, 'OK, yeah,' just so they'd go away and let me get on. And then she'd come back. 'But I want a hat with it, love.'

I remember going home one night and taking all the stuff in from the van. I was sure that I'd lost something or that a couple of things had been stolen. Finally, I thought, 'Jesus, I can't do this on my own any more.'

Don't get me wrong, I was really happy about the way it was all going, really happy, but I needed help. So Dave said he'd start coming down to the stall to give me a hand. Also, I needed him to take the money as I didn't like having cash on me when I was leaving the market.

By this time Mary Connors, the traveller that I had struck up a friendship with at the start, had started to come to the stall a lot, almost every Saturday, and I'd started to recognise her, affectionately, as Gypsy Mary. She knew everybody. 'Whatever I do, they'll follow,' she used to say. I knew that Mary was a bit of a queen bee, so I believed her. And she'd also taken to looking out for me: 'You've got to be careful with her,' she'd warn me about some other traveller. 'Don't give her this,' she'd say. 'Don't give them that.' She was full of good advice, was Mary.

She was kind but with a tough heart, you know. So there was an element of the 'If I do this for you, you do that for me' sort of deal. 'Don't charge me what you charge them, and I'll get you more business,' she'd promise. You wouldn't mess with Mary. She had six daughters, and every Christmas or Easter, or whenever there was a celebration, she'd have dresses made for the youngest ones. So, to be fair, she had bought quite a lot from me. Dave had even been down to a site she was living on in Manchester to deliver dresses to her. He used to come back and say that Mary and her family always made him feel welcome.

Mary's youngest – Josephine – must have been about eighteen months. Josephine was adored by all the family and Mary used to buy loads for her. But the thing I remember most about Mary's girls was that every one of them was stunning: they were all tall and slim, with long, flowing hair.

I hadn't seen her for a while, and then one day at the end of January she turned up at the stall. 'Our Mary's getting married. She's been asked for,' she said, 'and I want you to do the wedding dress.'

'Oh God!' I thought. My stomach turned over. It was January and the First Communion season hadn't really kicked in yet, but it was about to. I'd done a wedding dress for a cousin of mine, but I wasn't sure I wanted to do weddings as a business thing. I didn't really want to do adult dresses at all. I was quite happy doing the little ones. I'd even taken the cut-off age down from seven to six after all the gypsies started asking for bigger dresses. Anyway, I could do the kids' stuff with my eyes shut by then, because I knew what to do and where to get everything, but I really didn't want to do big ones.

Also, I liked the idea of having my weeks free and not having to be on the stall until Saturday, so that I could really concentrate on new designs. I loved studying to find new styles and it was great having time to have a really good look through all my history books. I'd study the costumes in them for hours, looking at every detail and the different braids and edgings, working out how I could apply all that fine decoration to my designs.

I'd also spend days at the library, using their computers and searching the internet. Once I found some old hand-drawn patterns from the seventeenth and eighteenth centuries, so I printed them out and took them home. I worked out how to scale them up, inch by inch, and made them into little kids' outfits.

Every night I'd sit and cut or sew, and I wouldn't go to bed until I'd finished something, making everything look as perfect as possible and as near to the styles in the books as I could possibly get them. Thinking back, they were quite amazing. I really liked Henry VIII's style of clothing, and I remember looking at the big flat hats he used to wear, and those tunics. I loved those, the shape of them – how they were straight but then gathered at the bottom, like a little skirt, because he was so fat. It was just the way the fabric flowed. I remember looking at a picture of him in one and thinking, 'That'd be lovely for a kid.'

So I made one in ivory velvet and designed a little coat to go over it. It was for a little girl and it looked really nice. It was so satisfying for me to do the kids' clothes and try things out with the other girls that worked with me. Some of the ideas made it, some didn't, but it was brilliant having the time to experiment. I really enjoyed that part of my job.

But this was Mary asking. She wouldn't take no for an answer and I just felt that I couldn't let her down. 'I've got to do this somehow. I've just got to do this wedding dress,' I thought to myself.

'Yeah, all right,' I said. 'What colour?'

'White!' she said, casting me a funny look, as though I was thick.

Mary had brought a picture in with her. It was a bride wearing a dress with long sleeves, a tight sweetheart bodice, nipped in at the waist, and a really big meringue skirt. 'OK, I said, that's fine.'

Only, Mary wasn't going to leave it at that.

'I want it a lot bigger,' she said. 'Three times the size.'

'Bigger than that!' I said. I couldn't believe what I was hearing, but I said OK, just hoping it wouldn't come off.

'I've got a deposit here. How much will it be?'

I told her I didn't know how much it would be. I'd have to have a think. Like I said, I'd never done a wedding dress to order before.

'Look, just give me a price. Tell me a price. Just give me a price, go on, give us one,' she kept on.

'I really do *not* know what it will cost, Mary,' I kept telling her. 'I haven't done a dress that big.' But she just wouldn't leave it. Eventually, I was so exasperated that I blurted out the first price that came into my head, even though I knew it was way too low.

'Tell me your best price and I'll give you a deposit right now,' she said, apparently not having heard the price I had just given her.

'I've just told you my best price, Mary.'

'And I want crystals on it, real crystals. Lots of them,' she said, putting her hand in her bra and pulling out some money. Then she started to walk away. As I watched her go, my head was spinning – I hadn't factored crystals into the price I'd given her. Then, just as she was about to disappear around the corner, she turned and shouted, 'Oh, and I want a big train on it, love, like that,' pointing to an imaginary train behind her. 'About thirty feet.'

I called her back. '*How* long do you want your train?'

'About thirty feet,' she said again.

'Thirty feet!' I said, looking at her, surprised at the way she seemed to imagine that was a perfectly normal thing to ask for. I didn't think she quite realised how long that would be. 'That's about from here to there, Mary,' I shouted, pointing all the way along the path that ran by our stalls.

'Yeah,' she said. 'That's it.'

'Well, it will cost you more,' I came back, hoping that she would think again.

'Ah, go on now! It's only a bit of material,' she said and was gone.

The next week she came back to the stall with young Mary and six other girls in tow. 'I've got Mary and some of the bridesmaids for you to measure.'

'So you want bridesmaids as well, do you, Mary?' I said.

'Yeah, I told you. Eighteen bridesmaids.'

'*Eighteen!*'

'Yeah,' she said. 'And her cousin's getting married the week before and she's having a 100-foot train, so I want our Mary's to be 107 foot now.'

I laughed and pointed right towards the very end of the market.

'Yeah, I know, it's going to cost me a bit more,' she said, dead straight-faced.

The wedding was at the end of April. This was the end of January, so I was looking at making nineteen dresses in three months. 'Oh my God,' I thought, when I worked it out. 'That's just impossible.' But I had taken the deposit and I just couldn't say no to Mary. I wouldn't – young Mary was so excited about the dress. Which, of course, was turning out to be absolutely nothing like the picture her mum had shown me.

That week I remember just sitting at home. I sat for ages and I couldn't think about any of the other orders I had. I came close to telling Mary that I couldn't do it and offering to give her the money back. Then it occurred to me that because Mary knew so many people, if she told them I didn't do it, there was a good chance that it might ruin my reputation with the other travellers.

But what really persuaded me was young Mary's excitement about the whole thing. I couldn't stop thinking about this young kid getting married, and how it was all booked, and how she thought she was going to have the best dress ever with this massive train.

It took me that whole week to work out in my head how to start. At first I just couldn't understand what she was asking for. I'd never seen a wedding dress anything like that size. I kept thinking, 'That girl's got a lovely figure. Why would she want something this size? It's ridiculous.' Eventually, I thought, 'I'm wasting time here. Just do it. You've just got to go for it. Just do it.'

I couldn't buy a commercial pattern because there weren't any for a dress like that. So I looked at all my costume books to see how they pulled the skirt fabric into the waist. Also, young Mary, whom I'd measured by then, had a 24-inch waist. And she wanted the best satin, not any thin fabric; it had to be Duchess satin, which is really heavy. But that's what I reckoned the Victorians would have used, so I looked at the way they did it and copied it. I also knew that there was only so much fabric I could fit into a tiny waistband.

Then I started to think, 'Where am I going to fit this dress?' I couldn't do it in the market. So Gypsy Mary came to my flat. She'd usually come with young Mary and three of her other girls in tow – two of the older ones who were going to be bridesmaids, and Josephine, always Josephine. Quite often she would end up staying all day at the flat, making tea and cooking dinner for everyone so that I could carry on making the dresses. Mary was always telling me stories about traveller culture. I was fascinated. I began to look forward to her visits.

'This dress has got to be fantastic,' she'd say. 'There are people coming from all over to this wedding, from America, everywhere. There will be 500 people there, so it's got to be really good.'

The pressure was ramping up, but the good thing was that I could count on Angela and Audrey to help me. We had another Audrey helping at that time too. So there was me in my flat, with Mary and the kids, the two Audreys working in their houses and Angela in hers. Everyone worked on different bits, and then I would collect them all and piece them together at my flat. The girls also did the bridesmaids' dresses. That's how I'd worked out was the best way to do it, because there was physically not enough space to fit all these dresses into my flat. Especially that wedding dress.

The fabric was sixty inches wide, which is the widest you can get, but that still wasn't quite wide enough, so I had to fathom how to stitch panels together to get a fuller effect. I was working on a dressmaker's dummy, but the skirts were so heavy that it was bending over. Every time I tried to put the underskirts on, the dummy collapsed. I thought of every way I could to try to make it work.

I went back to my books and had a really good look at the Victorian crinolines. They were all held up by big whalebone cages, so I thought, 'I'll make a cage out of stiff fabric and steel strips, and if I have some going this way and some going that, it should carry the weight.' But it collapsed: the steel wasn't strong enough.

I even tried making a sample on a smaller scale, and it seemed to work, but when I tried it bigger, it didn't. God, when I think of all the ways I tried to get around it. I remember one morning seeing the dummy all bent over and doubled up. Finally I decided to try it on one of the girls, and it was actually OK. On a body it was sticking out exactly as I wanted. It worked.

And then there was the train.

In my head that was going to be the easy part. After all, as Mary said, essentially it was 'just a long piece of fabric'. But it wasn't easy at all – and it wasn't just one long strip of fabric, either. It was thick satin and I had to do it in panels. Now, after trying to fit the huge, heavy skirts on to the dress, here I was with this massive train having to go on the waist as well. Can you imagine all that having to be supported by this tiny girl's 24-inch waist?

The train was so heavy it was pushing the dress forward, so I had to devise something to make it come out and over the dress. I went back to my books and decided that a bustle – a frame often used to support heavy fabric dresses in the 1800s – might be the best solution. It was trial-and-error time again.

Dave, as ever, was amazing: 'Come on, you can do it,' he'd say. 'You know you can do it. You'll work it out.'

'I can't.'

'Yes, you can. I'll help you.'

And he did. Dave always helped me make things happen.

The funny thing is, I get so many calls from people today asking how I make the dresses – 'How do you do this bit? How can I make my bodices stay like that?'

'You chancer!' I want to reply. 'It took me years to work all this stuff out. Do you think I'm just going to tell you over the phone in two minutes?' But, of course, I just politely tell them that it's best that they work it out for themselves as every design is different and our dresses won't be the same as theirs.

We put the bustle under the train so that it kept the fabric up and off the back of the dress, but as soon as the girl moved in it the dress bent back in again.

Then Mary came in to see her daughter's dress one day. She wanted more crystals on it, and I was still buying them retail as I didn't know a supplier. So I bought two packets of Swarovski crystals – about 3,000 of them – which seemed like loads, and scattered them all over the dress.

'Oh, no, that's not enough, Thelma,' she said. So I got some more.

Another day, young Mary looked at the dress. 'I want something round the edge of the trail,' she said. 'I want some edging.' Of course, she didn't want to pay any extra for it – her mum, Gypsy Mary, was a good teacher in that respect. So I sat there night after night, stitching the edge of this train with organza and crystals – all 107 feet of it.

Finally, it was done and it was really, really heavy. In the end, I thought, 'I've done what I can and that's what she wanted. If it collapses, it collapses. There's nothing I can do.'

But it was me who collapsed. I got really ill, probably with exhaustion. Then I got bronchitis.

Mary turned up at the house one day when I was not at all well. 'Thelma,' she said, 'I want you to do an outfit for my other daughter.'

'I can't, Mary,' I said. 'Honestly, I'm just physically not up to it.'

'Oh, it'll be an easy one,' she said. 'The wedding dress is nearly done now.'

So I ended up having to do another outfit for the after-party as well. Those three months of my life were hell. I remember sitting there thinking, 'I will never ever make another wedding dress so long as I live.'

Dave and me were invited to the wedding, but we couldn't go as it was in Peterborough and it would have been impossible to get back in time to do the market the following day. I remember the day the family came to pick up the dresses. It was the afternoon before the wedding and I'd worked right through the night making sure it was perfect, and at about four o'clock Dave put everything in their van. As they left, Mary called me to one side.

'Don't tell anyone what the dress is like, or the colour of the bridesmaids' dresses,' she whispered. 'And don't mention where the wedding is.'

'OK, Mary,' I said. 'That must be the hundredth time you've told me not to tell anybody anything.'

'It's just really important that no one knows about the wedding,' she said again. But it wasn't until some while later that I would come to realise why secrecy was important to her.

When the door closed behind them, I just sat on the end of the bed. I felt loads of things, but mostly glad that the dress was complete, and relieved that it was gone and out of the house. I didn't have the same happy feeling that I got when I finished the kids' dresses. I felt inadequate, to be honest, because that dress just wasn't good enough. It wasn't perfect. Even when it was finished it still wasn't the way I wanted it, but there was no more time to do it. All the same I was happy knowing that young Mary was so thrilled, and her mum was so proud of her in it.

Even now I smile when I think about that bloody train. In the end, we'd had to roll the train up on a pole, like a scroll, with a handle at either end, so that they could carry it to the church and then roll it out and put it on when they got there.

That day, sitting on the bed, I could still hear Dave talking to them outside. Finally the van door slammed shut. I put my head down. I could feel my body sinking into bed. 'This must be how you feel when you die,' I thought. But I can't remember what happened after that, because I slept for two days.

Someone had told the local paper about the wedding dress and its huge train, so the next time I saw it was in the paper. They'd photographed it from above, and you could see this tiny little figure at the altar and the train just going on and on and out the church door.

I must admit, when I saw it there on the page it did look good – even though it would have looked a lot better with a smaller train – and I started feeling a slight sense of achievement. It felt good to know that finally, despite everything, it was out there. It's funny because, looking at it now, young Mary's dress itself isn't even big. It looks more like one of our Communion dresses.

I suppose that most people would think I was mad to carry on doing all that, but I was just so determined to rise to the challenge. Mary had pushed me, then pushed me further than I ever felt it possible to go, but also, in a way, she got me started doing what I do now. So I have a lot to thank her for, not least for teaching me about the travellers' way of life. I'd still be doing the kids' clothes if she hadn't asked for that wedding dress. And all the extras that went with it.

And there was another reason for wanting to do right by Mary. All that time she came to my flat when I was making that first ever gypsy wedding dress, which she had pushed me so hard to do even when I hadn't wanted to, and which had nearly killed me, we'd got to know each other. We told each other things and we'd become friends.

After the wedding, everyone was talking about young Mary's wedding dress, as well as the after-party outfits and bridesmaids' dresses we had made. Because the travellers all go to the same events and all know each other, news travels quickly. So then I started getting phone calls asking, 'Is this the woman from Liverpool who makes the dresses?' Then they'd say, 'Can you make me one of these, love?' It would be all make me this, that and the next thing. 'I'll send you the money, love.'

So now I had all these phone orders, which meant I had to call the travellers a lot too, and this is when I really found out that gypsies don't communicate like settled people do. For a start they never, ever return your calls. And, on the rare occasion that they pick up, they'll tell you that they don't know who or what you're talking about. 'Oh, I don't know her, love,' is what they'll say, even though you've talked to them face to face a hundred times before.

I used to think it was me, and that I was always taking their numbers down wrong. But I was slowly getting to know them and to understand how the travellers talked to each other, so I started doing it their way: passing messages on. 'Do you know so and so?' I'd ask one of them. 'Can you tell her there's something here for her?'

So quite a few of the travellers had started coming back to me and I got quite close to them, hearing all about their lives and listening to their stories. Most of them revolved around the next wedding they were going to. It was just 'wedding, wedding, wedding' the whole time.

Another two of Mary's daughters got married the following year. Of course, I made their dresses too.

4

The Tale of a Love Gone Bad

My divorce from Kenny was nearly complete, but the dealings around the financial side of it were becoming somewhat acrimonious and there was a lot of to-ing and fro-ing. My now ex-husband thought that because I'd been bankrupt and my share of marital assets had been swallowed up I didn't deserve much. He wanted much more than I thought was fair, but unfortunately everything was still in his name. Had he forgotten that I had worked the whole time we were married?

It was early 1998 and me and Hayley had moved into a small flat, as I couldn't afford for us to live in the marital home any more, and I was working on the stall at Paddy's. One day

Hayley came home and said, 'Mum, my friend said his mum and dad have just bought our old house.' I couldn't believe what I was hearing. Kenny was still seeing the kids every now and again, so I knew a little of what he was up to. But I wasn't prepared for this.

Even though I knew my name was not on the legal documents, and that I probably didn't have a chance of having a say in any sale, it still felt like a slap in the face. And the idea that someone we knew would be moving into our home was hard to take.

Apart from everything else, I was bloody angry. I called Nancy, a friend of Tracey's who was working at a solicitor's office at the time: 'Can you believe that our Hayley has just come home and told me that our house has been sold?' I said. She said I should get in touch with a solicitors' firm who'd dealt with divorce cases that she'd heard were good, as I'd need someone who specialised in that area. They were called Morecroft Urquhart and everyone said they were the best family solicitors in Liverpool.

I went down to see them and met with a Mr Freeman. I told him everything that had happened and how I'd heard that the house was going to be sold.

'Oh no it's not,' he said, picking up the phone.

'But it's not in my name,' I told him, trying to explain more, while he sat with the phone perched on his shoulder, waiting for the person at the other end to answer.

'It doesn't matter,' he said. 'We are going to put a charge on that property. He can't sell it without you knowing.'

After twenty-four years of marriage it looked as though I was entitled to something after all. 'Jesus Christ,' I thought, 'there's someone on my side here.'

But Kenny hadn't sold the house. He'd been really fly and done a house swap instead. The deal was already done and so we had to put a charge on the house that he was now in – their old house, which meant going to court.

I was on benefits then, and because I was claiming income support for me and Hayley I could get legal aid. There's no way I could have afforded to take Kenny to court if I wasn't getting that.

The case was at Liverpool Family Court and it was taking a lot longer to sort out than I had hoped. Kenny was getting angrier and angrier the longer the case went on. He'd sit in court and just glare at my solicitor, who had got his measure. One day as we were walking out along the court corridor after a session, Mr Freeman said to me, 'If looks could kill, I think I'd be dead.'

We had to find out how much money Kenny had got from the house swap. This meant he had to declare every penny he had and show all his bank books and receipts to the court. The trouble was, every time he showed his bank statements, it seemed as though he was skint. His account was completely cleared out. It was as if he was saying: 'Well, if it's not there you can't have it.'

A few days later, Kenny called me. 'I need to see you,' he said. I decided it would be a good idea to meet with him as we might finally get things settled. But when I met with him I found out that what he really wanted was to stop at nothing to make my life hell.

'I'm telling you now,' he warned, 'you'd better back off. If you don't, just you see what I'm going to do.'

As soon as I could get away from him, I called the solicitor and told him what had happened. I wasn't scared – it had been a long time since Kenny had had that effect on me, and I knew I hadn't done anything wrong, but Kenny's anger worried me. Mr Freeman was dead calm. 'They all say things like that,' he said.

'But he will make my life hell,' I told him. 'He means what he says.'

He laughed. 'Every divorcing person says that.'

I wasn't so sure.

A few weeks later, there was a loud buzzing at my flat door at about half past six in the morning. It was so early that I sat bolt upright. 'Bloody hell,' I thought. 'Who on earth is that?' I stumbled to the intercom and pressed the buzzer. 'Who's that?'

'Merseyside Police.'

'Oh, God,' I thought. 'Hayley.' She'd been staying at a friend's the night before, as I knew I was going to court the next morning and we lived quite a long way from her college. I pressed the buzzer and told them to come up.

When I opened the door, five plain-clothes coppers were crowded round it. 'Thelma Madine?'

'Yeah?' I said.

'We're here to search the property.'

'What for? What do you mean you're coming to search the property?'

'We have reason to believe that you've used stolen cheques.'

It was weird but I just had an instant flashback to a police programme I'd seen on telly. 'Have you got a search warrant?' I asked, as if I knew what the hell I was on about.

'No, we haven't. We don't need one.'

'OK,' I said. 'Then I suppose I'll have to let you in.'

So they looked everywhere. In every room. One copper started taking things out of the cupboards and was sitting at the kitchen table writing stuff down in his notebook. 'What are you looking for?' I asked him. 'Tell me what it is and I will get it for you.'

Then Dave arrived. He had come to pick me up to drive me to court. He walked in looking a bit bewildered, and I tried to explain what was going on, even though I wasn't quite sure myself. 'I know him,' he whispered to me, looking at the policeman sitting at the table. Dave said he thought it was someone Kenny knew as well.

'I've got to go,' I said. 'I'm in court today.' It was the last day of the divorce hearing, when they make the financial settlement, the decision of who gets what, and I *had* to be there for nine o'clock.

'You're not going anywhere. You're coming with us,' said one of the coppers.

'But I've got to be in court!' I said, getting a bit panicky.

'Well, we didn't know you were going to court,' he said.

I just looked at him. 'Phone Mr Freeman and tell him what's happened,' I said, turning to Dave as they walked me out of the door. I was taken downstairs and put in a car with two of the other policemen.

'I can't believe this is happening,' I told them.

They led me into a room at the police station and questioned me for hours. They asked me if I wanted legal help, but I said that I didn't need it as I hadn't done anything wrong. It turned out that the cheques that they were on about were the ones that Kenny and I had signed when I was bankrupt, the ones I'd had to use to get the fabric and things for the business when everything was in Kenny's name.

'Is this your writing?' they asked, pointing at this old cheque with 'K. Madine' in my handwriting scrawled along the line at the bottom.

'Yeah,' I said. 'Yeah, it is. But I thought Kenny was OK with me doing that.'

They pulled out more, pointing to the writing at the bottom. 'Is that yours? Is that yours?'

It was all being taped. I'm going, 'Yeah. Why are you showing me these? This is all stuff for the business. He was running the business.'

Three weeks later the case was dropped. I wasn't going to jail for writing forged cheques. But there wasn't any sense of relief. About a month later I got a letter from the DSS asking me to go in for an interview. 'What's all that about?' I thought, as I put the letter back in the envelope after reading it. I couldn't work it out at first, as I wasn't signing on.

Anyway, I went in on the day they asked me to and was taken to a room where two people interviewed me. They just sat there and listed loads of dates, stopping to ask, 'Were you working on such-and-such a date?' And, 'On such-and-such a date were you doing this?'

'No,' I said. 'If I was meant to be working on that date, what was it I was meant to be doing?' So they would go through the whole thing again, like a pair of robots: 'On such-and-such a date were you ...'

They asked me: 'Is that your business at the market?'

'No it's not,' I said. 'It's Dave's business.' The thing is, they knew the business was in Dave's name and that I worked on the market stand on Saturdays, as I'd declared that. You are allowed to work so many hours a week, and they take some money off your benefit for that. And though it may have seemed as though we were raking it in, it took a while for us to start making any money off the stall. Cash flow was always hard at the start and the materials were so dear. Also, it took me a while to get the pricing right and we were working all hours to keep everything going.

I admit that I had been signing on when we started and I didn't tell them. I know it was wrong, but I would not have been entitled to legal aid for my divorce if I wasn't on benefits and I couldn't have afforded not to have it. And in the beginning, before it started getting dead busy, I didn't know what I was going to make on that market stall from one weekend to the next, and I still had Hayley to look after. I'd never had to look after her on my own before, and I was always thinking, 'What if I don't make any money this week?' I felt I needed the income support – it was a security blanket.

But I should have stopped claiming benefits earlier than I did. I just couldn't bring myself to tell them that, so I denied it. The next thing, I got a letter from the DSS telling me they were going to take me to court.

All the time, I couldn't help wondering if Kenny had played a part in all of this.

By this time I was making a wedding dress for Mary's other daughter, so Mary knew what I was going through as well. I talked to her about it – Mary was a good listener. She knew people who had been in similar situations, and she was good at making me feel like the worst wouldn't happen.

She brought me a little card, one of the ones you get from Catholic shops. It was in a Cellophane wrapper and had a little medal on it. It was a picture of a prince walking along the sand. You could see another set of footprints alongside his, as though someone was there – even though no one was visible. I think the message was, 'There's always someone there for you.' Travellers are very religious. I'm not, but I knew it meant a lot for Mary to give that to me, and her little card did make me feel better. I still see Mary from time to time at other traveller weddings, and it's always lovely to have a catch-up. She was the first traveller that I got to know and she's right at the heart of my strongest memories of Paddy's and my first gypsy customers.

By then, everyone who worked near me on the market, and some of my regular customers, knew about the court case and the DSS investigation. Markets are like that – everybody knows everybody else's business. And people always seemed to be claiming on the side, which is why the inspectors used to turn up there.

One day there was a right commotion at the top of Paddy's indoor bit and everyone stopped and tried to look as we could hear this big fight going on. We all looked at each other and thought: 'Oh, let's run up and have a look.' It was hysterical, just like being at school. This woman who had had a stall on the market for years was standing in front of these two guys, effing and blinding like nobody's business. The stalls near hers were empty, as people had scarpered as soon as they got the news that the inspectors were coming through the market.

They had just asked for her National Insurance number. 'Are you claiming Carer's Allowance for your mother?' one of them asked.

'Indeed I am not!' she shot back. She sounded indignant and dead funny.

'You shouldn't be working as we know you're claiming for your mother as a carer,' the other said. They kept on like that for a few minutes. Then she exploded.

'My mother's *deaaaaaad!*'

They looked terrified, said something about getting it wrong and scurried out of the market as fast they could go. I think they thought she was going to kill them. I think she probably was.

There was always a bit of a fight or something going on at Paddy's, someone being robbed, or the police, the DSS or the Trading Standards turning up. Everyone had known someone who was in my position at some point and who had been investigated for something or another. 'Oh,' they'd say, 'remember so-and-so? Well, she got caught and only got six months' community service. That's the worst you'll get. Don't worry.'

The investigation carried on for the next two years. All that time I was working on the market. Mary was still coming by and I was starting to get quite close to a lot of my other traveller regulars. I loved listening to their stories, which all came back to one thing: weddings.

After doing Mary's daughters' dresses, I had wondered about going into weddings seriously as part of the business. The idea of it was always popping up in my head. In the end, the decision was made for me.

One day Pauline called in a bit of a state. She'd been working on her own little stall in a shop selling kids' stuff, and I used to supply her with some christening and Communion dresses. She was crying. 'Oh Thelma,' she said, 'the shop's burnt down.' I knew Pauline didn't have any insurance. I felt sorry for her and tried to make her feel better.

'Paul, you know, one door closes and another one opens,' I said. I understood what it was like to feel that you had lost everything, but I also knew that you could pull it all back, no matter how desperate you might feel at the time. 'Think about it,' I said. 'It will be all right. Everything will be OK.' But within a couple of days she told me that all the stock had been ruined.

There was only one thing for it. 'Come back and work for me, Paul,' I said. 'We can do Paddy's together on Saturdays.' And that's how I ended up working with Pauline again.

A while later Pauline and me were catching up one Saturday morning. 'You know that stall I used to have in that shop,' she said, as we were putting all the little stands out for the christening dresses. 'There was a big room upstairs.'

'Yeah,' I said, slowly remembering the shop and that it was on a busy road.

'Well, the shop a couple of doors down, the one on the corner, is the same, and he's selling it,' she said.

'Yeah, but I can't afford that, Paul,' I told her. 'I can't afford a shop.'

I was interested in having a look, though. So I asked to go and see it the next week.

From the minute I got there I started planning out the space in my head: I could see room for a little office bit in one corner and a machine in the other. The room upstairs was really nice and big, and when I looked at it the wedding dresses idea came back to me. If we took this space we could have a proper go at them. Pauline was right – this shop was perfect.

Finally, the fella who owned it said he would agree to lease it to us rather than sell it. But he wanted £250 a week. There was no way I could have afforded that, and I didn't want to get in trouble and end up being bankrupt again. I was good at a lot of things, but money was never one of them.

But I was determined and came up with a plan: I kept thinking about how things worked at the market, and then I thought that I'd ask a couple of the other stallholders to come in with me, like concessions, so we could share the rent. I knew there was a woman who made cakes, another who did jewellery, and a fella who did these going-out clothes. With us making the dresses, that would make a nice little business, I reckoned. They were all keen to give it a go, so I decided I could take the shop on. I knew the business was coming.

We moved into the shop at the end of 1999. It still had its old sign up, with the name 'Nico' above the window outside. I thought about changing it but I liked Nico, so we kept it. We moved all of the stock we used to take to the market, but the space was so big that the kiddies' dresses looked a bit awkward and bare sitting there. I knew we needed to start thinking about the wedding dresses as soon as we could.

Pauline and me went to a few wedding trade fairs to have a look at what was out there. I had to find other stock so that I wasn't having to make every dress myself. If I was going to do this as a regular thing, there was no way I could make everything. It would be the end of me.

We came across this fella who sold corsets. They were amazing, really lovely. He did them in all the usual colours – black and red, pink. 'Do you do white ones,' I asked, 'like for weddings?' He showed me some that he had, but they were quite dear – £250 each, and that was cost price. They were all different designs and really nicely decorated, but I knew they weren't exactly as my customers wanted and I knew I could do something better.

The fella said that he wouldn't take an order for anything less than six as they were made abroad. So I asked him to send me some. Then he showed me a really big skirt that he had. It was made with loads of netting but it had this edging along the bottom that you would never put on a skirt, like a plastic boning. It made the hem all twisty and curly and I just thought, 'Ooh, I like that,' because I could see exactly how it would look on a much bigger dress.

'Can you do a wider skirt, around five times the width of that?' I asked him.

He looked at me as though I'd lost the plot. 'It *is* really wide. It would be impossible to make it wider,' he replied, still looking at me in a funny way.

'No it's not,' I thought. I knew it wasn't.

When the corsets were delivered I took one to the market and hung it up. It hadn't been up for long when a girl came in and ordered one. She was a traveller and said she wanted it for going out. I hadn't really thought about the price, so in my mind I did what you do in business and doubled what I'd bought it for. It was covered in diamanté, but even then I thought there's no way I can charge her £500.

'I'll do it for you for £350,' I said. 'Just give me a deposit of £100.' She wanted a short skirt to go with it. 'Oh, go on then,' I said, 'I'll throw the skirt in.'

So the next week I made a big net skirt with the twisty stuff around the hem and put it together with one of the corsets. Straight away a traveller girl came up and said she wanted it for a wedding. It was her perfect wedding dress, she told me.

I gave her what I thought was a fair price but even then I felt I was pushing it, so I agreed to do it for less, as I wanted her to tell her friends about us.

Then, a few weeks later, this other girl came in and looked at the corset and skirt I had on the stand. 'I want that,' she said, just pointing at it.

'The same shape?' I asked her. 'Yeah,' she said, 'but I want a big butterfly here.' She was pointing to the front, making a butterfly shape with her hands. She wanted a corset in the shape of a butterfly, not just a pin on the side or anything.

'A butterfly?' I said.

'Yeah,' she said. 'And I want another butterfly on the back. And I want a big skirt, a really, really big skirt.'

And I thought, 'Yeah, I know what you want. You want a *really* big skirt.'

I built up a good relationship with the corset supplier and he'd said to me that if I ever wanted anything special done, just to let him know. So I had to phone and tell him that I wanted a bodice with a butterfly all done in crystals, the Swarovski ones.

When the corset came I looked at it and just thought, 'Oh no.' He'd kind of stuck a butterfly on it. I knew that wasn't what she wanted. So I took off what he'd done, and did my own butterfly. I covered the bodice in Swarovski AB crystals, the ones that look clear but change colour in the light. I made the skirt as full as I could, so that it looked a bit *Gone With the*

Wind, and I also made her a veil to match. It was absolutely gorgeous. I mean, looking back now, and comparing it to the size of some of our recent dresses, it probably wasn't that special, but she was over the moon with it, really over the moon.

I put in a few more orders with the corset supplier, but they kept coming back wrong. Also, they were taking ages and all these traveller girls that were coming in wanted them within weeks. That's another thing about most of my customers – they don't understand that someone's actually got to make these things. They think you can rustle up ten of these dresses in a day, as if by magic.

I knew that I had to learn how to make these tops. I studied one of them closely but couldn't really work out how it was done. I realised that although they were expensive, the only way I would crack it was by taking one apart. I unpicked the panels and had a good look. I thought I could tell what they were made of and all the different bits of material I would need to make them work. But I wasn't getting it. The boning wasn't right and the shape was awkward-looking. It was back to my old trial-and-error days. I soon found out that if the stitching's too tight the corset edge curls up and doesn't sit right. If it's too loose the corset just slips around.

It took me about two years to finally get those corsets right. And now I don't let a corset leave the workshop if it is not absolutely perfect – just as though someone has rustled it up by magic.

'There's no way in this world I can sit here all day making corsets,' I thought. 'I just don't have the time to do that.' I was constantly thinking about how we could make the business work without making the corsets.

But, like a lot of things in life, it turns out that the answer to the problem was staring me in the face. There was a café next to Nico's, and there were always some Iraqi guys hanging about upstairs. They all used to meet there and congregate around the back. Now, our car park was round the back, and ever since we moved in there had been a lot of trouble over that space.

Every time we'd pull up there would be four of their cars parked in there, so we couldn't get in. We had arguments with them all the time. I even got their wheels clamped. I did everything, but it didn't stop them. God, when I look back, there was murder over those parking spaces. So I used to have to go up the stairs and shout at them.

'*Whose cars are they?*' I would scream. They'd all just stand there and look at me like, 'Whatever' – like I was daft. It was a nightmare.

But after a while another guy took over the café and he was much nicer. He was all, 'I'm sorry, I'm sorry. Just come and tell me when it happens.' So he kind of sorted the problem out and we became friends.

He started coming into the shop and having a cup of coffee with us. He was just dead nice.

One day he came in and brought this lad called Alan in with him. 'My friend is looking for a job,' he told me. 'Have you got anything for him?'

'What can your friend do?' I asked. He told me he had been a tailor in Iraq.

'Go on, then,' I said. 'I'll give him a try. I'll give him a month's try-out.'

So, in came Alan. Straight away, I thought, 'He's good, this lad. He knows what he's doing here.' So I wanted to try him out on the corsets to see if he could do them. He tried, but he kept coming back to me, saying, 'Not very good, not very good,' and he'd go back and do it again and again. He really put the effort in, did Alan. By the end of the month he brought another one down to me. It was near enough perfect.

Alan also managed to get the one thing that had always thrown me – the right moulding material. After working on the corsets for a while he said he could get this stuff from a supplier he knew that he thought would work. It did. Alan was really creative too, and he'd come and show me things and say, 'I can do this shape', or 'I can do that.' So with Alan and Pauline now on board, Nico was well and truly in business.

5

The Tale of a Nightmare Come True

It was 2001 and the DSS case was dragging on. It was now over two years since they'd sent me that letter. I'd actually managed to deal with the pressure of it hanging over me and, on the whole, had managed to put it out of my mind and just get on with the business. But, finally, they set a date for my trial.

It would take place in the third week of November, at Liverpool Crown Court. I was relieved, though obviously still worried – the fact that it was being held at the Crown Court meant it was very serious. But at least it would all be sorted one way or the other and I could finally put a lid on the whole episode and get some peace.

Although we were making things at the shop, we still had Paddy's. So I told my market mates about the court date and they were all behind me, saying that they would come to court and support me when they could.

I was being charged for claiming benefits while running a business – or false accounting, as they called it – between June 1995 and July 1997. There were five charges in total and the case had been brought against me, the barrister said, because 'they were acting on information by an informant'. Someone had told them I was signing on while working, basically. To this day, I swear it was Kenny Madine, but he's always denied it.

But, no matter who or what had got me there, the fact is that I did what they said I did, though not for as long as they claimed. I signed on while I was working, and that's the reason I was in this situation.

During the trial, which went on for five days, the courtroom was packed with people from the market. They came every day. The thing is, they're all dead loud. One of the women, Mary Hughes, has got the biggest heart and a mouth to match. She shouts the whole time, just shouts, everything. Mary didn't actually work on the market, but she used to come to the market every Saturday with her friend Josie Berger and they became regulars at my stall and the others around me. I'd made dresses for Josie to send to her nieces in America and got to know her through that. They were both great, really good laughs, real salt of the earth. You always knew when they had arrived at the market, as before you even set eyes on Mary, you could hear that voice from one end of the market to the other. I was glad they were there for me, and Josie actually took to the stand as a character witness. Baby Mary, Josie and Mary Hughes came every day.

After the first day the judge took to making early calls for 'The Madine Supporters' Club' – that's what he called them – so that they were quietly settled in the courtroom before proceedings started.

The first person that the prosecution called as a witness was Ruth, the woman I had gone into 'business' with a few years before – she had agreed to testify against me. She told the court how I had been making clothes in the garage at the family home and then selling them in the little stall we had set up in Petticoat Lane. I wanted to shout out, 'She set up the stall, not me!' She said that she had 'fronted' the shop for me, 'a friend she was trying to help'. But from what I remember, Ruth only ever helped herself. In fact, she'd tried to help herself to my business.

They called another couple of people to speak against me, including the fashion agent from Belfast, who told them that between 1995 and 1996 it was Ruth she'd dealt with on the business side of things.

My barrister explained that I had been in a bad way money-wise at the end of that year, just after Kenny left, and that I had had to get a crisis loan to be able to heat the house. That was why I had started signing on in the first place.

Then it was time for me to take the stand. The lawyer for the prosecution passed a book over to me and asked me to have a look at a page with dates and phone numbers in it. They were trying to prove that it was my orders diary. 'Is this your book?' he asked.

I looked at the page and then flicked the pages back so I could see the front of the book. The cover said, 'This book belongs to Ruth Prince.' That was Ruth's name before she got married. 'This isn't my book,' I said.

'Oh, isn't it?' said the prosecutor. 'But it was in your flat.'

'It might have been,' I said, 'but it says it belongs to Ruth Prince.'

He changed the subject. He asked me to turn to another page and read out an entry that was in there which said 'sailor suit'. I told him it was for my daughter.

'For your daughter,' he laughed, sarcastically. 'A sailor suit for your daughter? How old is she?'

I told him she had been about 13 at the time. It was gorgeous, that sailor suit. It had rows of gold buttons on this dead smart navy blue jacket – it looked a bit like something Princess Di might have worn, a bit eighties, but in a good way. Hayley loved it. I remember it like I made it yesterday.

When I stepped down off the stand, my barrister said, 'We're winning. Everything's going great. I don't think we need to call any more witnesses, but if we do, who do you think out of your proposed people we should get to do it?'

I thought, 'Well, who's not going to do me in?' I knew that Dave would be good, and Tracey – my eldest daughter – wouldn't worry about having to take the stand. She'd be the best person to explain the way life was at the time and how hard it had been for me.

So Tracey was called, and she was brilliant, putting them straight about my relationship with Dave and how tough things were in the house and with money. She did so well and I was really proud of her. The whole thing seemed to be swinging in my favour.

Then it was Dave's turn. The prosecution asked him some questions about the business and he started spouting nonsense. It was awful. If you've never had to take the stand in a big courtroom before, you'd never know how horrible it is – it's like being under a spotlight or on a stage and it could easily throw anyone. I suppose that's maybe the point.

Dave wasn't coping with it at all. He was panicking and started saying this stuff about a dog. Everyone was looking at him, bemused, as if to say, 'Sorry? A dog? What dog?'

Then the prosecutor said sarcastically, 'What dog? Oh, I see, the dog was running the business.' I sat there, hiding behind my hands, sinking lower and lower into my seat.

The look on Tracey's face, and on Hayley's face ... All of us were sitting there thinking, 'Oh my God. What's he doing? What's he going on about?' Dave had totally lost it.

They asked him all about the wholesale side of the business and wanted to know where he bought all the stuff. He told them that he got it in Manchester and that he didn't remember everything because he was an entrepreneur who 'did bits and bobs'! Everything Dave said from then on was like another nail being hammered into a coffin. My coffin. It was unbelievable, like we were all sitting watching a car crash in slow motion.

After Dave's turn in the dock, the court session was adjourned. When we got out into the hall, my barrister looked at me and sighed. 'We're losing it, Thelma. We're going down.' I thought, 'Oh God, does he mean me? Am I going to jail? What does he mean?'

So, despite my beliefs it was Kenny trying to get me sent down, it was Dave, the man who means the world to me and who would do anything for me, who was actually making it happen.

Of course, this being Liverpool, there's always a laugh to be had, especially when life seems to be taking a dark turn. It was the Friday, the last day of the trial. The jury was sent out to make its decision and we were all asked to leave the courtroom.

All the women from the market were with us in the café. We spotted this woman sitting on her own, and she seemed upset, so Mary Hughes went over to her. 'Are you all right, girl? Come have a cup of tea.' So she joined us and told us what she was there for. She was getting a divorce, she said, and it was turning out to be terrible. Mary piped up, 'Well, love, it can't be any worse than hers,' she said, nodding her head towards me. 'Her bastard husband's trying to put her in prison.'

The woman looked at me, then turned back to Mary. 'It's worse than that,' she said, looking back into her coffee cup.

'Why?' Mary asked.

'I've just turned up for the divorce and he's turned up in a dress, fur coat and high heels!'

I spluttered out my coffee. 'No way!' I said.

'Go on!' said Mary.

The woman pointed to someone sitting behind us. One at a time we walked past and had a look, and right enough, there he was, this woman's ex-husband, in a flowery frock, a wig, a fur coat and slingback shoes. He was about six feet four!

'All right,' I said, laughing, 'yours is worse.' We all had a good laugh then.

A few minutes later the court was called back into session, so we filed back in to hear the verdict: 'Guilty.'

I was found guilty on four of the charges, but the fifth charge was dropped. They had accused me of claiming for eighteen months, but my barrister was able to prove that I had only been doing it for twelve. I was found guilty of claiming £9,000

that I wasn't entitled to. I was told to come back in three weeks, when I'd be sentenced.

Those three weeks felt like three years. It was unbearable, all the waiting, not sleeping. The next week I had to go for probation reports. I'd never been in trouble with the police before, and I had admitted that what I had done was wrong and that I had carried on claiming money longer than I needed to. I had admitted that I deserved to be punished.

The probation officer, a woman, asked me: 'What would happen now if everything went wrong? Would you do it again?'

'Oh God, no way,' I said. 'Never again.' It's a question I still ask myself today because I often look back and wonder why I kept doing it.

But this woman was dead nice. 'You'll be fine,' she told me. 'I'm going to give you a favourable report because you've never been in trouble before and I don't think you'll re-offend.' She told me that I would probably get community service.

And so it arrived. The sentencing date: 10 November 2001. I walked into court surrounded by my family and friends from Paddy's. There was Dave, Hayley and Lee, her boyfriend, and Tracey and her boyfriend Peter.

Me and my family were all dressed up, as the plan was to go for a big meal that night and celebrate the case being over. We all settled in the courtroom. The judge took his seat and everyone looked over. You could have heard a pin drop. I could only hear my heart beating and was hoping that no one else could.

'Thelma Madine,' he said. 'Stand up.'

I got up and stood there looking right at him.

He said something about me living the high life and how I had wanted to carry on living the high life. He said that I had been used to getting things and wanted to carry on …

I wanted to say, 'What, for £100 a week, are you kidding me?' but you just have to stand there and listen to what he has to say.

I can't remember exactly what he said after that, but it was something along the lines of: 'This is a high-profile case and we are going to make an example of you. This is not a victimless crime …'

'Yeah,' I thought, 'it's a high-profile case because it's been in every frigging paper.' The *Liverpool Echo* covered it in loads of detail: they loved the scandal. But at least they used a nice picture of me. It was lovely, that photo – I've still got the report cuttings from the newspaper.

One of them reported exactly what the judge said next: 'You are an intelligent and articulate woman who has demonstrated an ability to run these businesses …'

'God,' I thought. 'That man knows me.' He carried on: 'I bear in mind that your claims were not dishonest from the outset, but your financial position changed. Your claims were dishonest and cynical and these monies went towards maintaining your relatively lavish lifestyle.'

Some people who owed 50 or 60 grand were getting twelve months. But he said this was a high-profile case. He said I wanted to keep living the high life – but I had no heating! He said I knew exactly what I was doing. He said he was going to make an example of me.

And then he said the things that would change my life forever: 'Thelma Madine, I sentence you to twelve months in prison. Take her down.'

Everyone gasped. All I could hear was Hayley crying. Then she started screaming, '*Mum! Muuuuuum!*' The policemen took me down the stairs. 'Shit,' I thought. 'Shit!' That's all I kept thinking. 'Shit, shit, *shit.*'

They led me along the corridor to this little room with a glass screen. My family were allowed down to see me. But they weren't allowed in. They could only talk to me for two minutes through the glass screen. Then I was taken to a cell.

I sat there staring at God knows what, waiting for Dave and the kids to come and tell me it wasn't happening, that they were coming to take me home, and that we were going out for that meal after all. Then Dave appeared at the cell window. He was having to hold Hayley up. I remember seeing Hayley's face – and she's always been the strong one. Dave was white. They all were.

Hayley had broken down completely. Tracey looked shocked. I'll never forget their faces. None of us could believe this was happening. It was like a film, something you watch on telly. It wasn't real life. It wasn't our lives. It was horrible.

But I never got a chance to see them properly, as the next thing I knew I was being taken away. I was led out of the court cells and into one of those prison vans with the little windows in. They were taking us to Styal women's prison in Manchester.

When I stepped up into the van, I looked in and saw these cages along each side. I remember thinking it was like that film *Con Air* with Nicolas Cage, when all the prisoners are sitting on the plane but the really dangerous ones are kept in cages. This time they contained a few sorry-looking women.

And here was I, walking in all dressed up like Joan Collins. I looked at the cages and thought, 'That must be where they put the bad girls, the serious offenders.' Then they opened one up and put me in it.

'Over here, love. Have you got a ciggie, love?' one of the women whispered to me through the cages. She went on like this the whole way from Liverpool to Manchester. 'Have you got a ciggie? If you've got any give us one 'cos they're going to take them off you anyhow.'

I couldn't take it all in. I was stunned. 'No,' I kept thinking. '*No. No. No. No.*'

I felt like it wasn't happening to me, like I was watching someone else. It was all a dream – but it wasn't. I knew it wasn't. I always have this dream now where I'm running down the street with no shoes on, and it brings back that feeling I had sitting in that prison van. Sheer panic. Overwhelming fear.

Being taken down is the worst feeling ever. That doesn't even go half way to explaining what it feels like. If someone had given me a chance to go home and pack some stuff, to get my head round it a bit first, I could have handled it better. But when you are sentenced there is no chance to prepare or to say goodbye.

I honestly believe that when they send you down and take your freedom and rights away from you right there and then, with no explanation of what's going on, it is so that it shocks you to the core, so that you never commit a crime again. I kept thinking that this was what the punishment was, that it was a warning, and that any minute now they'd come and say to me: 'We're giving you a suspended sentence, but now you can see what will happen if you ever do it again.'

That van ride to Styal only lasted about an hour but it felt like a lifetime. As we drove along London Road I tried to look out of the window and caught a glimpse of the top of the shop front. The Nico sign was all lit up in Christmas lights, twinkling away as if nothing had changed. I felt sick.

Getting that shop had made me feel as though my life had turned to a new page. I had felt as though I had reached a different stage in my life, as though everything was falling into place for me and Dave, for the kids, for the business and for Pauline.

Not any more. I was in this cage. No rights, nothing. My life was over, finished. I couldn't even phone anyone. They'd taken my phone off me.

I remember it was about four in the afternoon and it was pitch black outside as it was winter. All the Christmas lights were on. I couldn't see properly, but I could see the shapes of people as the van drove by and loads of red lights, and I could feel everyone rushing about outside, doing normal things, getting their Christmas shopping.

There were three other girls in the van. The one next to me was a druggie. She was all, 'Miss, miss ...' I tried not to listen to her, let alone look at her. They were all shouting or whispering at the same time. 'This is Hell,' I thought.

We got to the prison and they led us out of the van in a line. The first thing they do is take you to see the prison doctor. They tell you to strip, to take everything off, and then they search you all over – they check your whole body. Then you get a shower and another check-up and you are told to put your clothes back on.

After a bit of paperwork, I was led up to my cell. I was sharing with another woman who was just sitting on the bed when I got there. There were bunk beds and a toilet in the corner. I couldn't take it in. As soon as I got in, the woman turned to me and said, 'I'm awfully sorry but I have to go to the toilet.' So now a stranger was shitting right next to me. 'I can't do this,' I thought. 'I can't do it.'

Someone came along and shut the cell door. 'Oh God,' I thought. My heart was pounding so hard, I couldn't breathe. 'Oh God,' I kept saying to myself. 'Oh God, I can't breathe.' The cell stank. I thought I was going to collapse. I looked up and felt some air coming through the window. There were bars on it, though, which meant the window could only open about an inch. I ran to the window to try to breathe in some air.

My cellmate must have seen the colour of me and she pressed the buzzer. The door was clanking, like it was being unlocked. A female prison guard walked in and looked around. 'What?' she snapped.

'She's having an attack here,' said the woman.

The guard looked at me. 'What's the matter?'

I was gasping, 'I can't breathe. I can't breathe.'

'Sit down. Calm down,' she said. Then she walked out of the cell, leaving the door open. I felt a slight relief. But a couple of minutes later this other woman guard walked past. She stuck her head in. 'What's this door doing open?' she said.

'She's having an attack,' my cellmate said.

'Tough!' she barked and slammed the door shut.

I tried to calm myself down. I started talking to my cellmate to try and take my mind off it all. I was in shock. I sat there for hours and hours feeling as though I was going to die, thinking, 'What's going to happen? I don't know what's going to happen.'

You're allowed a phone call, and so that night I was able to phone Dave. The girls were there but I couldn't speak. They were sobbing. It was terrible. Really, really bad.

I remember Dave saying, 'Don't worry, it'll be fine. Don't worry.'

I went back to my cell trying to take everything in – the other women, the stairs, the rows of cells. It was quiet. I tried to get to sleep, so that I could block everything out, but of course I couldn't even shut my eyes.

The next day I had to go and see these officers who try to make a plan for you, to give you some idea of what you will be doing while you are in prison. They were all saying, 'I don't know what you're doing here.'

For the first two weeks I was in that cell with the other woman. That part of the prison is called the Wing and it's where all the newcomers are sent, but it's the worst part. It's where the very bad ones stay: murderers and people like that. No one was coming to let me out, I knew that now.

I did my best to keep it together, and I got letters every day from my family and friends. They kept me going. Prison life is boring. It's all about routine, a bit like being in hospital. I called Dave and the kids every night, and that helped, even though I'd feel down for a while after. I was still in shock, but it didn't feel as intense and I got into the routine. I did what I was told to and got on with it. The woman I was sharing with was quite nice, and we got on, so that helped too.

After those two weeks they put me in one of the separate buildings in the prison grounds where low-risk prisoners are sent. They are called the Houses, and that's exactly what the building I had been put in was like – a big house. Some of the rooms slept two, some three and others four. There were around twenty or thirty of us in each House. My room-mate was Donna and we became good friends.

They asked me if I wanted to work and I told them I was desperate to do something. So they put me in the kitchen, serving and organising the food. It was a good job and it kept my mind off everything.

I started to get on with a lot of the girls, and after a while I was part of a group of prisoners who were put together to look out for the most vulnerable girls in there, to protect them from being bullied and things.

I knew that a lot of bullying went on and that some women like to take control and act like the queen bee, like those women in prison dramas on telly. I could stand up for myself so it wasn't a problem for me. Though there had been this one woman in our House who had been there for a few years and acted like she ruled the roost: nobody could sit in her chair and she always chose what was on telly, that sort of thing. She was getting a bit annoyed at the fact that I was popular with the other prisoners.

We didn't have any hairdryers or straighteners, but I'd worked out that the iron did the trick, so I was in the laundry room once trying to straighten my hair with the iron. This woman walked in and said, 'No. We don't do that here,' and flicked off the switch at the wall. I looked at her, looked at the wall and switched the iron back on again. 'What's it to do with you what I do?' I said. 'Everyone else might do what you say, but I won't.'

She looked totally shocked that I'd talked back to her and that I wasn't scared. She never bothered me after that; in fact she was always trying to be my best friend. It was pathetic schoolgirl stuff.

I did four months in prison in the end. Now that doesn't sound like a long time, but believe me, it felt like a lifetime, especially over Christmas. Being in there, away from the kids and Dave, was a very lonely time. I had worked out that the real punishment when you're sent to prison is not the prison; the punishment is being taken away from the people you love.

I'd also realised soon after I got there that the only way to get through it all was to turn the situation around. I had to find a way of coping, to stop feeling hopeless, so that it didn't seem so bad.

From the moment you are sent down in court, you're immediately aware that you have no rights, that everything you take for granted in life – the right to choose, to have a say, to be free, to spend time with your family, to have a fag, to phone your mum – has been taken away from you. The bottom line is that the jail is in control of you, and you're there to do what you're told.

Now, at first, this was the most shocking feeling for me – you can't begin to imagine how that feels. Yet, strange as this might sound, it was that feeling that began to give me hope. I began to quite like it. For the first time in as long as I could remember I was no longer a wife, a mother or a boss. I had no responsibility. I was simply Thelma.

It made me think: in real life you may be a millionaire, but the minute a prison door slams behind you, you have the same as everyone else in there – nothing.

6

The Tale of Life Within Prison Walls

The four months I served felt like four years. Every day was like a lifetime but I had no choice but to get on with it. And so that's what I did. 'I may not be able to do anything about this, but I'm not going to let this beat me.' That was something that I said to myself over and over again.

I was dreading Christmas in Styal, and knew I'd miss Dave and the kids a lot. Then I remembered how much I'd always hated Christmas Eve, with all that running around for presents and food shopping. It was tradition for everyone to come to ours for dinner, so I'd always be busy frantically planning and cleaning the house from top to bottom. Most years I'd never get to bed before four o'clock in the morning. Every Christmas

I promised myself 'next year will be different' – but it never was. Until now.

So I just got into the swing of Christmas Day at Styal, and as none of us had any responsibility whatsoever we ended up behaving like little kids and actually having a good time. There were only twenty girls in our House, so we made a little buffet dinner. In the evening we ended up playing truth or dare and running about knocking on doors and having a laugh.

One of the girls in our House said that she had been saving a little out of her wages each week to buy some goodies so that we could have a party. Another girl said she had brought some Hooch. She handed me a cup with a little bit of alcohol in the bottom. It didn't look very much like Hooch. It turns out that some of the prisoners had made it themselves – from what I do not know, and I'm glad I never found out. Their 'Hooch' did make me a bit tipsy, though.

Christmas came and went. I had been in Styal for five weeks. I know I keep saying this, but it felt a lot longer, as though it had been a year or something. But then my life had changed beyond belief in that short space of time.

In the first week of January, just after Christmas, I was moved to an open prison, Drake Hall in Staffordshire, and Donna was being moved there too. At that time it was a women's open prison, but I think it's a closed one now. To move us there, we had to travel in one of those secure vans, the same type of van I was in when they took me away from Liverpool Crown Court the day I was sentenced.

The difference in the way I felt getting into that van then, compared with the utter horror that I had felt walking into the one a month or so earlier, was amazing. Donna, who was in her early twenties, about the same age as my Hayley, made me laugh a lot on that journey. I knew then that I would get through this; I had started to get my head around this awful situation.

While I was away, Dave kept the shop going. Pauline was there taking the orders and Dave was looking after the business side of things. My daughter Hayley had also started working in the shop by then. We hadn't begun to do wedding dresses, but the First Communion season was coming up and so all everyone had to do was to keep the business running.

After a few weeks I started to draw out the designs for the Communion dresses. I would send them to Dave with letters telling him exactly how I wanted them to be. Dave would take them to Pauline and tell her what I wanted. Pauline knew the whole Communion dress process inside out. But then Pauline can do anything. She could sell ice-cream to Eskimos if she had to, so I knew that Nico was in the best possible hands and I didn't worry about it.

Naturally, when you go to prison, one of the first things that everyone asks you, and the first thing you want to ask them, is why you are in there. Donna was sent to prison because she and her boyfriend had been involved in a fight with a guy and a girl, and the man had ended up getting stabbed and killed. It was Donna's boyfriend who pulled the knife and he got five years, but Donna was jailed too as she was there and part of the fight. She got the same sentence as me – twelve months, even though in her case someone had died.

There was this other girl who asked if she could borrow a lighter from me. 'What are you in for?' I asked.

'Oh, it's stupid really. I didn't do it,' she said. I'd realised by then that almost everyone who was in prison with me was 'innocent' and that most of them 'didn't do' what they were supposed to have done.

'Oh, right,' I said. 'So what was it that they said you did?'

'Arson,' she said.

I'd just given her a lighter, and I sat there watching her playing with it, thinking, 'Shit.' Someone told me that that was her second time in for setting fire to things. But, actually, you could tell that she wasn't really right in the head. She shouldn't have been in prison. She needed psychiatric help.

Quite a lot of the girls in prison obviously need professional help and you can tell that they are not wilfully criminal. Some, you get the feeling, are definitely sly, but there are others that you just can't fathom. In general, though, when you spend time talking to all these people, people that you wouldn't want to know or even give the time of day to outside prison, you begin to see that they were once normal and just going about their lives until something went wrong that they maybe couldn't cope with. It was how they'd dealt with these situations that had turned out the wrong way.

There was one woman that I used to talk to who was really nice. She had two budgies in her cell. That is how you can tell a lifer, because they are allowed to have a budgie. 'Did you get two life sentences?' I asked her one day.

'No, but one of the other girls got out and left me her budgie too,' she said. It was really sad. I think she had been sentenced to about twelve years. She didn't tell me what she was in for. There are lots of people in Styal who won't admit to the crime they are convicted of, which means they don't have any chance of parole and have to serve their entire sentence.

But this woman had a girlfriend. A lot of long-term prisoners form relationships with each other and when I first went to Drake Hall I was quite shocked to see lots of women walking around with their arms round each other. I was quite naïve about it at first, and whenever I saw women being affectionate with each other I thought, 'Oh my God, they're lesbians.' But when you've been there a while you don't even think about it, and you can see that for a lot of women it's about companionship and just wanting a hug.

So this woman's girlfriend told me that the budgie lady was in for murder. Her story was that she came home one day, when she was seven or eight months pregnant, and found her husband messing about with their little girl, who was about three. Apparently she went and got a shotgun, came back and shot him, and that was it. They said that if she'd just killed him right away she would have been sentenced differently, but because she'd thought about it enough to go and get the gun it was premeditated. She lost both her kids – they took the baby away from her as soon as it was born.

There were a lot of women in prison because they had killed their boyfriends or husbands. Quite a few were in for drug trafficking, too, even though most of them say they didn't know they had drugs on them. There are also some cases that you just can't believe people have been locked up for, like the girl who got six months for lying on a form that she had signed when applying for a job in a bank. Well, apparently she wrote something that wasn't true and they sent her down for it.

There was another woman who had been driving a coach that crashed. Two of the children on board were killed, and she was done for dangerous driving and got two years. It was terrible, but she hadn't intended to hurt anyone. At the other end of the scale was a woman who worked in the prison's hairdressing school. You could go to the hairdressing department and have training if you wanted, so that you could leave prison with a skill, or you could spend your wages there, getting your hair done. So I went there to get my hair bleached, and this woman washed my hair. When I walked out, another prisoner told me that she was a lifer who had killed her two kids. 'Oh, she's just been washing my hair!' I thought. It kind of gave me the creeps. Usually people who commit crimes against kids are segregated for their own safety, but this child killer was as large as life, working in the prison hairdressers.

But after talking to the women in there, I really did begin to change my views about people and about who and why we judge. The area where Nico is in Liverpool is next to a red-light district, so we are always seeing prostitutes hanging about there. 'Dirty smackhead,' I used to think when I saw one of them, and if they asked me for a cigarette I'd bark, 'Go away, go get a job.'

But I spent a lot of time talking to women whose lives had been wrecked by drugs when I was inside. There was this one girl who was very well spoken. She came from Liverpool and lived not far from my mum. She was obviously very intelligent, but you could tell she was a drug addict, as she was so thin and grey-looking. She had a little girl and told me she'd had a job in a government office, a good, well-paid job.

She went to a party and took a little bit of cocaine, then a bit more, and a bit more, and before long she started taking it just to help her get through the day. She ended up being a full-blown drug addict on heroin, and stealing to feed her habit. She lost her house, her little girl, everything. But then a lot of the girls in prison are addicts. I was sitting in a cell once and saw a poem someone had written on the wall about heroin. It said something like, 'I need you but I hate you and what you've done to me ...'

When I first went to prison, I thought, 'I shouldn't be here.' I just didn't accept it. 'I'm above these people, I'm not like them,' is what I used to say to myself. Although I can't really pinpoint exactly what it was that changed my mind, I started to realise that that wasn't exactly true. After listening to all these different stories, I started to think that, really, I was no different from anyone else in there; these people weren't from some different form of life from me. Everyone has their story to tell, and each one is different.

I would find myself looking at some of these poor young girls whose lives were a cycle of prostitution and drugs. 'Bloody hell, would I have done that?' I thought, if I had been a young kid from a different family and been told by my mum to go out and be a prostitute to earn money, like some of these girls had been. 'Thank God I had a good upbringing and a mother and father who cared for me,' was a thought that often crossed my mind during my time in prison.

But then there were a few other smart girls from good families in there, which just goes to show that you might think you're above everything because of where you come from, but you're not.

Quite a few travellers end up in prison and, a little ironically perhaps, I think their background has a lot to do with it. Only not in the way you might think. They are brought up to be so confident, and are so adored by their parents, and I think it makes them feel slightly invincible, like nothing's going to touch them. But being inside is no big deal to many convicted travellers. Whereas lots of people might hide the fact that they'd been in prison or wouldn't want to tell anyone, they just talk about it matter-of-fact. Prison is part of life for a lot of them.

Drake Hall was an open prison and it was also a working one. You had a job to do in the day, but you were encouraged to learn new things and take night classes in your free time.

Every day you had to work at your allocated jobs until four o'clock, but after that they didn't make you do anything. So a lot of the girls just didn't do anything, and seemed quite depressed, sitting in their rooms in the evenings. But I went to the gym every night and made sure that I had things to do. I was always going off to some class or another, just to keep my mind and body working well.

I was interested in taking computer lessons as I'd always wanted to learn how to use one for the business, but I'd never had the time. Now I had a lot of that, so I was delighted to be put down for basic classes.

They gave us all a simple little test to see how good our English was. One of the girls next to me was sweating, she found it so hard. The test was honestly so simple that it was heartbreaking to see this girl panicking.

I was told that I couldn't do computing as it was for people who had failed the test and needed educating. But I spoke to the woman who took the classes and she arranged for me to get lessons on the computer in the mornings, as long as I worked in the afternoon. Now I'm good on the computer and I can do Excel and things. Before I got out I was about to learn about databases, but I never did. I've still got a mental block about them, and even to this day I avoid doing them.

Workwise you had the choice of what you could do, whether it was in the kitchen, the laundry or the gardens. There was also a sewing room.

So when they asked if we had any particular skills, I told them I could sew and was sent to the sewing room. When I turned up for the first time there were some Scouser women sitting at the machines: 'Weren't you in the papers?' one of them asked. 'Aren't you the woman who makes the Communion dresses?' another said.

'Yeah, that was me,' I said.

'Well, you're just sewing in here,' she said. 'You won't be doing anything creative.' We were doing things like sewing hems on bags for cheap shops, just straight sewing, basically.

Donna and I wanted to be together, so I told her to come to the sewing room too. 'But I can't sew,' she said. 'I'll teach you,' I told her. So in the afternoons we both took our places in the sewing room.

By then quite a few people had been told who I was, as some of the women had read about me in the paper when I did Mary's daughter's dress with the 107-foot train. The woman in charge of the sewing room asked me all about it and I told her what I did, and about the Communion dresses and the things I had made at Paddy's. She told me that they were thinking of doing a project for the upcoming Queen's Golden Jubilee. They wanted to make dresses of queens through the ages, which would be used in a parade.

I just thought it was so funny. I mean, it was as if I'd made that project up myself – I was in prison, and here I was being offered my perfect job!

The only problem was that they didn't have the equipment to make patterns, and so I offered to have some things sent in. Obviously there are many things you're not allowed to receive as a prisoner, but the woman was really kind and said they could be sent to her and that she would bring them in to the class.

I was the most popular woman at Drake Hall after that, because we had to do a lot of research in the library and, as I was allowed to take someone with me, everyone wanted to be my friend. So I taught a few of the girls the whole process of making dresses, from the research to the finished garments. I never got to see the parade, though, as I had been released before they put it on.

While I was inside the divorce settlement came through. The court said Kenny must pay me a certain amount of money or they would take his house. He would have to sell it and give me what I was due.

A few weeks later Kenny got in touch, asking to come and see me. I told him that he was the very last person I wanted to see and not to come. Then my eldest, Kenneth, came to see me. 'Mum, will you let my dad come and see you? It's really important; he has to talk to you.'

Because it was my son asking, and Kenneth said he would come with his dad, I said OK. So, as planned, Kenny came to prison to see me. We talked politely for a while, and he protested that he had nothing to do with my being in prison.

'Whatever, it's over,' I said to him. 'You can't threaten me any more. I don't want to talk about it. And, anyway, what do you want to talk about that's so important?' I asked.

'I just want to know: will you marry me again?'

Honestly, I could not believe what I was hearing. Kenneth also looked at him in total disbelief. 'Behave, Dad. Behave,' he said. I never really got to the bottom of that crazy notion and I didn't want to upset Kenneth by pushing it any further. Maybe Kenny just felt guilty. Who knows? All I knew was that I didn't care any more.

I can't tell you how lucky I feel to have the family that I do. We all got through this, no matter what's gone on between me and Kenny. My mum and dad also stood by me, but though my mum came to see me a lot my dad never visited. 'I can't see my daughter in a place like that,' he said.

And then there was Dave, who did everything he could to hold our family together. My girls and my mum would go round and see him a lot when I was in prison. In fact, my mum used to go and see Dave about three times a week, to cook for him when he got in from work. My mum was just brilliant, and so was he. He was strong for my girls and they could come to him for anything. They still do now. Our family became stronger then, and their pulling together gave me a lot of hope.

The thing is, I've always thought, when men are in prison their families usually stay together, because it's the woman who keeps it all going. But it's all too apparent in women's prisons that when mothers are locked up everything can so easily fall apart.

I do still think that lots of the women I met in prison are good – even those who are in for murder – but some of them have taken abuse for so long that they just snapped. Who's to say what you or I might do in that position? And, watching it from the inside, it seems as though women prisoners are more heavily punished than men, in that they're more likely to have their children taken away and put into care. You see so many kids coming in with foster-parents during visiting time. It's really awful.

Not seeing my kids every day was the most painful thing about being inside. It was the only thing that really, really hurt me. They used to write me little letters when I was away, and I brought them all home with me afterwards. Hayley even sent me a little diary. She'd written something in it every day, like,

'I love my mum', or 'Keep strong for us'. I appreciate my kids more than ever now.

And they would also tell you that I'm a completely different person. I'm so much calmer than I used to be, and I don't insist on everything having to be perfect at home. Little things, like the house having to be sparkling clean all the time, don't matter any more. I'm so much more relaxed.

As Drake Hall was an open prison, I was allowed out once a month, towards the end of my sentence, between nine and four o'clock. Dave and the girls would pick me up in the morning at about nine and bring me back around teatime. I can't tell you how much I looked forward to these days, even though it was hard to have to go back at the end of them. But because they meant so much and really gave me something to look forward to and work towards, I made sure that I just got my head down and got on with my sentence as best as I could.

When you're sentenced to a specific time, you are meant to serve that. But everyone has the chance for parole and to be released with an electronic tag after serving part of their sentence. But they don't tell you how long that part is going to be, so you never really know how long you will have to serve and when you're going to get out. My official release date was December of the following year, as I would have served the twelve months by then. I knew I was due to get a tag at some point, but when? The other thing is, even when you get told your tag date, it doesn't mean you're going to get out that day.

MARKET TREASURES: From Little Bo Peep to Russian and Victorian princesses, these travellers' little boys and girls looked as though they had stepped out of the pages of my costume books.

PEEK-A-BOO: My right-hand woman Pauline on the stall at Paddy's Market in 2000.

FAMILY FAVOURITES:
(Clockwise from top left) Me and my brother Tom with our mum and dad on a trip to a Christmas Grotto in Lewis' in Liverpool in 1957; an Easter outing with my dad in 1959 (check out my neat hat and gloves); me and Kenny on our wedding day at the Church of the Good Shepherd in Liverpool in 1970; with my daughter Hayley at Butlins in 1981; Showtime! Me and my brother Tom at tap-dancing school in 1956. He was a brilliant dancer.

THAT'S MY GIRL: Kenny and me, with his sister holding my eldest daughter Tracey on her Christening Day.

FUN IN THE SUN: My son Kenneth and daughter Tracey, on holiday in 1974. Looks like we went to Butlins again!

QUEENS OF SUMMER: I made all the dresses for the Lydiate Rose Queen Festival in Ormskirk in May 1988. My daughter Hayley (back row, second from the right) was a train-bearer.

HERE COMES THE BRIDESMAID: Hayley, aged 3, as a bridesmaid in 1983.

HAPPY NEW YEAR: Dave and I take a break in the Lake District at the start of 1997.

PRETTY AS A PICTURE: My youngest daughter Katrina in 2007.

WAITING FOR THE TRAIN:
The first wedding dress I ever made, for young Mary Conner, the daughter of my Paddy's Market friend Gypsy Mary. It had a 107-foot train. Making it nearly killed me!

GIANT SKIRTS AND TONS OF SPARKLE:
(Top) One of our Irish brides having a fitting in the workshop. She was delighted with her dress but wanted the skirt even bigger. (Bottom) This traveller bride wanted every inch of her corset covered in crystals.

RECORD BREAKER:
This dress was made from hundreds of metres of netting, tulle and satin. It was 40-feet wide, weighed 12 stone and had over 3,500 Swarovski crystals on it.

VICTORIANA RULES: A 'night-before' wedding outfit for one of our Rathkeale brides.

managed a 16-minute dance, but she had to stand still as her dad waltzed around her to *My Girl* by The Temptations. Then Michael took his place and Carly sang Shania Twain's *You're Still The One* to him.

Carly had met her landscape gardener husband, Michael, as a youngster. They became childhood sweethearts when they hit their teens and soon decided to marry.

They spent several months organising their dream wedding, which cost around £40,000.

Proud dad Frank said: "The dress cost a lot, but it was worth every penny to see Carly happy."

Fortunately, Carly didn't expect her hubby to carry her over the threshold. And to avoid excess baggage, the dress didn't join them on their honeymoon in the Canary Islands either!■

By Susan Dickeson

closerstories@emap.com

Fortunately, Carly didn't expect her hubby to carry her over the threshold

OUR FIRST EVER BIG FAT WEDDING: This dress was featured in publications all over the world and is still talked about on the internet today.

QUEEN OF HEARTS: This is Nan, one of our beautiful Belfast brides, and her mini-bride (below).

READY, STEADY, PULLLLLLLLLL: Pauline and I help one of our brides, Mary, through a tight doorway on the way to church. (Right) Mary enjoying a glass of bubbly with her father Larry.

THE FUTURE MRS SWAN PUMPKIN: Larry's other daughter, Margaret, on her wedding day with her bridesmaids. At 25 stone, the swan pumpkin is the heaviest dress we've ever made.

HAPPY FAMILIES: Snaps of the Macdonagh family – one of the nicest families we've ever worked with.

THEIR DREAMS COME TRUE: (Clockwise from top left) A double engagement celebration for the Macdonagh sisters; our first prom dress, inspired by a Barbie outfit; the sunflower bridesmaid; this girl wanted an outfit with a Katie Price-style wedding corset; a feather collar adds the finishing touch to this engagement dress; this bridesmaid wore something blue; Bridget Ward's bridesmaids were a vision in hot pink.

So you have these meetings where nothing ever seems quite resolved. They call you in and say: 'You might be getting a tag then, or you might not.' Then they call you back and it'll be about something completely different. The wait is just terrible. I remember Donna being really upset because they told her she was very unlikely to get a tag because she was involved in a violent crime and she also didn't have an address to go back to. You see, you need to have a lot of things in place before they let you go, so they go out and check your home, to see that you've got one to go back to. As it turned out, Donna got her tag before I did, though we ended up getting out on the same day: Friday, 12 April.

It is a date that is etched on my mind. I was released at nine in the morning, and Dave was outside the prison waiting to drive me home. I was so relieved it was over. I'd had that whole court case hanging over me for five years. And every day during that time I'd wake up and it would be the first thing on my mind.

So, even though it may sound odd, when I went in to prison a small part of what I felt was relief, because the worst thing that could happen had happened. Now that sense of relief was the biggest thing I felt. I had the rest of my life to look forward to. 'From now on this is me,' I thought. 'I've no ties to Kenny any more. I don't have to fight with him and I don't even have to see him. I've got a man who loves me and I've got my kids.'

When we got back to the house, the kids all came round. It was the most brilliant feeling, but it was a bit surreal too. I also felt slightly insecure, as though I wasn't protected any more. It felt as strange as it felt good. It was going to take a while, I realised, to get used to being home. My freedom had been taken away from me just like that, and it had been given back to me in the same way. I was probably almost as shocked by that as I had been the day I was sent to Styal.

I suppose I was suffering a bit of an anti-climax, if you could call it that. Life in prison means sticking to a strict routine. It's difficult to imagine, but when you come out one of the hardest things is not having that routine any more, and having every-day control of your life handed back again. I was able to eat what I wanted, to take a bath when I wanted, and to just pick up the phone and talk to my mum when I wanted. That felt odd, and it took a while to feel like myself again. In prison you become part of a community and it makes you feel secure. So I totally understand now why people talk about being institu-tionalised – and I was only in prison for a few months.

I'd looked forward to my release day so much. I had a lot to look forward to, especially my family. But I couldn't help thinking about some of those other women, whom I'd spent that part of my life with, and who were left behind or had left the same day as me. So many of them were worried about getting out and what was next – maybe because their fella had gone off, or their kids had been taken into care. I was just so sad for these women who felt that they had nothing to go back to. I know that they did wrong and that, like me, they had to take the consequences, but life just doesn't stop being tough for some people. They really have no hope.

Then I thought of Donna. She used to say to me, 'Who's going to give me a job now?' Because when you apply for a job you've got to declare that you've been in prison. And that means that you know that you have no chance, and that they're going to give anyone else that job before you. All the women inside were worried about that.

So, on the day I got out, I kept looking around me, thinking, 'How lucky am I? I've got things to go back to and a family that loves me. I've got a job. I've got everything.'

7

The Tale of the Motherless Child

By the summer of 2002, my life had finally started to feel normal again and I was able to move on and get stuck back into the business. Nico was going well and we'd started getting more and more wedding-dress requests.

Margaret was only 15 when she first came to see us at the shop a few years later. She had long, black hair, bright blue eyes and an absolutely beautiful smile. She was such a pretty girl that you couldn't stop looking at her. She told me she was getting married as soon as she turned 16, which was only a few months away. Then I knew that she was a traveller girl.

We'd already made several wedding dresses for gypsy girls. They were getting bigger and more opulent every time. A few of them had made it into the newspapers, and some magazines had done stories on them too.

And so that's how Margaret knew about us. She was still a child, I suppose, but then all the traveller girls who came to see me at Paddy's were really young and I'd got used to it. I'd even started thinking of 20-year-olds as being a bit over the hill!

Working with our traveller customers on their wedding dresses wasn't as straightforward as it had been on the children's clothes and Communion dresses at the market. The big dresses took a lot of time, what with the fittings and the to-ing and fro-ing with the girls about the designs they wanted and all the extra details they were desperate to add.

We got to know all the girls and their families really well, but Margaret sticks out in my mind. I remember, so clearly, the day she came through the door; how excited she was. We all sat down and I told her about all the things she could have and then asked her what it was that she wanted.

I kind of knew the answer to that already: 'the biggest white wedding dress you've ever done'; 'the most crystals that had ever been on a dress'; and 'the widest dress you can do'.

I looked up from the sketchpad. 'Anything else, Margaret?'

'Just make me the best dress that's ever been made,' she said. 'I've got my deposit.'

'OK,' I said. 'We can do that.' But then Margaret wouldn't stop. She just kept adding things on. It was all, 'Oh and I want that,' and then, 'Oh, but I want this too.' She was just like any normal 15-year-old – she was just a kid.

Finally I looked at her and thought, 'She'll go on like this all day. This is a waste of time.' After she had asked for the corset to be completely covered in diamonds, and a pair of diamond-covered gloves to match, I put my hand up: 'Stop!' I said. 'Listen, Margaret, bring your mum in the next time, and we can all work it out together.'

'I haven't got a mum,' she said.

So I started drawing out her ideas for the dress and told her I'd post some more ideas to her the following week. The next day the phone rang. Pauline picked it up. 'It's that young girl from yesterday,' she said, passing me the phone.

'Thelma, I need to come back and see you,' Margaret said. She said she was going to come back up from London because she wanted this on it too, and now she wanted that … I kept trying to stop her, but she just kept going and it was getting into thousands of pounds' worth of extras. Finally I said, 'Margaret, I'm going to have to speak to your dad.'

She gave me his number. When he picked up I explained who I was and that I was a bit worried about how much Margaret was ordering and that it was getting into ridiculous money.

'Give her what she wants,' he said.

'OK, that's no problem,' I told him. 'But you do know she's going overboard and that she's telling me her bridesmaids' dresses are more like wedding dresses? She's asking for them to be just as massive as hers and covered in crystals and everything.'

'Fine. Just do it,' he said. 'Just give her what she wants,' was all he kept saying. I told him I'd need half the money up front as it was going to cost so much, and he said, 'OK.' The money came, no problem.

The thing is, travellers are just so crazy about their kids. They love them so much. I've never known a culture where people idolise their kids to that extent. I mean, it doesn't take much to work out that these men are tough, but the way they talk to their kids is really loving. They're always saying things like, 'Come here, my baby, come here, my baby girl,' and they are forever cuddling them and making them feel special. They are so passionate about the kids, especially their little girls. The mums and the dads adore the girls and focus all their attention on making their girls' dreams come true. That's why every gypsy girl's wedding day is such a big, big deal. And that's why they believe that their daughters should be allowed to have whatever they want.

Not all families let their girls go as mad as Margaret, though. There are restrictions, and some are not as rich as others, but every bride wants the best and every bride has to wear a dress that no one's seen before.

The weddings are also a bit of a status symbol within the communities. Travellers are generally very proud people and their weddings are a chance for the families to show how successful they are. They all work for themselves as well, so it's their way of saying, 'I'm doing OK. I can give my daughter the biggest dress, the most ornate dress.' They also get a sense of pride from knowing how much their daughters look forward to that day.

Even when the girls are just little kids – four or five, say – they bring them into my shop and say, 'She wants you to do her wedding dress when she grows up. You'll do hers, won't you?' Most gypsy girls start fantasising about their wedding dress almost from the minute they can draw.

The thing is, unlike most girls their age, traveller girls don't go out clubbing or to pubs or anything like that. The only things they go to are other travellers' Communions, weddings or engagement parties. They don't know anything about what goes on in the world of clubs and pubs, and they only get to meet potential boyfriends at traveller events.

That's why so many of them, like Margaret, are kept like little girls. Many leave school when they're about 11 or 12, because their mums and dads don't want them mixing with the other non-traveller kids or to be tempted into doing things that non-traveller teenagers do, like drinking or messing around with boys. From the age of about eight these girls are taught that their job is to learn how to cook, clean, wash and look after their siblings. They learn how to be homemakers.

I suppose it's also a way of keeping their children close to their community: by having the big wedding day and giving their girls everything they want, the girls will think their way of life couldn't be any better.

With Margaret it was even more the case, because she didn't have a mum. I mean, she was definitely spoilt, but there was something just so unique about her. She was very insecure and needed a lot of love, and when we were doing the fittings she'd turn to us and say: 'Do you think people think I'm pretty? Do you think people will think I look lovely?'

'Yeah,' I used to tell her, 'you're absolutely gorgeous.' She was a stunning girl, but she worried all the time about what people thought of her. 'Do I look thin?' she'd ask when we were fitting the dress on her. 'Will I look nice?'

This was very, very rare for a gypsy kid. I've never met one yet that was as insecure as Margaret was. Travellers bring their children up to believe that they are the best things since sliced bread, and that's why gypsy kids are so confident. You can see that from the way some of them talk on the TV. They're not shy and they find it easy to say what they think. Actually, come to think of it, they talk all the bloody time!

But Margaret was different. She was quite demanding, but underneath it all she was a sweet girl. Me and Pauline got really close to her, and one day, when we had finished a fitting and she was going home, she turned to me and said, 'Oh, I love you,' and put her arms around me. 'You'll come to my wedding, won't you? I need you there.'

In the end I started to feel as though I *was* her mum. She phoned me every single day and, no matter how busy I was, I always took the call. Not only did she want something different every time she called – more changes to her dress, a different colour for the bridesmaids – she'd be asking for things that had nothing to do with the wedding. 'Can you do that for me? Can you get this?' she'd ask.

Margaret was just so used to getting her own way, but then she didn't know anything else. You couldn't help but feel sorry for her, because on the one hand she didn't have a mum behind her all the time, but then on the other she was very spoilt and just wanted everything. She was crying out for a mother's affection.

Her mum had died not long after she was born. And it seemed as if her whole family – there were three sisters, a brother and her dad – cosseted her so much that she hadn't been allowed to grow up.

Every now and again, while we were in the process of making the dress, one of her sisters would call up and say, 'Take no notice of Margaret, she's a spoilt little bitch going on about what she should and shouldn't have.' They all loved her, but they could see that she was getting out of control.

Margaret would phone the next day and I'd say, 'Listen, love, you know you're pushing it. This is going to cost so much money it's going to be ridiculous. Your sister's already been on the phone.'

'It's OK, it's OK, I'll just talk to my daddy,' she'd say. She was like a baby, a pretty little baby that everyone adored. Her dad paid the bill, no questions. That, I soon learned, made him pretty unique too.

You could tell that the family all loved their dad, but that he was strict with them. With Margaret, though, I think he just didn't know how to handle her. I spoke to him a couple of times and he was really protective. It was like the memory of his wife was wrapped up in her. I trusted him, so we just kept on doing what she asked. In the end we weren't just making dresses – although we had six bridesmaids' ones to do too, as well as Margaret's – we were making a 15-year-old girl's fantasy become a reality.

'Do you think this will be the best wedding ever?' Margaret asked me when she came for her final fitting. 'Will everyone think I look pretty?' she said, as I laced up her corset.

'Tighter, I want it tighter,' she said, as I pulled the laces in. 'I want to look really thin.' She must have only weighed about seven stone. 'This is the best dress you've ever made, isn't it?' She was so excited. 'I want it to be in *OK!* magazine,' she said to me. 'Will you get them to come to my wedding?' I smiled at her. 'I'll try,' I said. 'That magazine's normally just for celebrities, but I'll try and get another one to come along.'

When all the dresses were finally finished, Margaret asked me and Pauline to come to London on the wedding day and put her dress on for her. I wasn't keen to drive all the way down there and take time away from the shop, but Margaret really wanted us to be there. 'My dad will pay you to come,' she said. 'Please come down. I really want you to be at my wedding.'

I thought about it: that dress had twenty-two underskirts, and if they weren't put on right either she or it was going to collapse. 'OK, me and Paul will come to the wedding,' I told her.

So we got organised and started the drive down to London. Then, when we were about fifty miles away from the hotel where the family were getting ready for the wedding, and where the reception was going to take place, the car broke down. We looked at each other: 'Oh my God, this can't be happening.'

We had Margaret's dress in the car.

We were going to have to abandon our car, as the AA couldn't send anyone out quick enough. After a few frantic phone calls, Margaret's dad sent someone to pick us up. When we finally drove up to the hotel it was ten minutes to one. The wedding was meant to start at one o' clock and Margaret hadn't even started putting the underskirts on. When we got there she was standing in the car park, waiting.

It took two hours to get the dress on.

'I want it bigger. Please put more underskirts on,' she asked me. But every time we put the skirts on she'd want them off, as they hurt her. They weighed a bloody ton. Margaret's dress was the biggest we'd ever done. It was massive.

'I told you this in the shop, Margaret,' I said to her, as we tried to fit them around her. 'I told you that if you wanted all these big skirts they were gonna hurt you.' She was just standing there in the middle of this dress. It was getting bigger and bigger. It was filling the room.

I had warned her at the time – and I tell all my traveller girls this – that these giant skirts are all very well when they are standing having them fitted in the shop for ten minutes or half an hour, but wearing them the whole day is a different story.

'Listen to me, Margaret,' I said. 'If it gets any bigger it's going to cut your hips to bits. You'll be crippled by the pain.'

We put a few more skirts on and told her to try walking, to see how far she could go. But she wanted them all on. 'I don't care, I don't care, I don't care, I don't care, I want them all on,' she kept demanding. She was used to getting her own way.

'OK, it's up to you,' I said, 'but don't say I didn't warn you.'

So we just kept going: eighteen, nineteen, twenty, twenty-one … Finally, we got the dress on. We smoothed out the last bit of satin and she was done: the entire room was filled with reams and reams of white Duchess satin, thousands of Swarovski crystals twinkling away. In the middle of it was Margaret, with her glossy jet-black hair, tanned skin, bright-white teeth and crystal tiara. She was like a living doll. She looked beautiful.

Only we couldn't get her out of the room.

We had to take most of the underskirts off again and try pushing her through the door. When we got outside, a bit of a crowd had gathered, so we had to take her around the corner of the building to put all the underskirts back on.

She was in a lot of pain and really sobbing by now. All the attention was too much, and her emotions had boiled over. Our dresses were a lot heavier then. We realised after a while that the traveller brides were always going to want them bigger, so over the years I've had to find a way to make them lighter.

But that day, me and Pauline just sat with Margaret for about twenty minutes, hugging her and telling her it was all going to be OK. I said that we should just leave all the underskirts off, but she kept insisting: 'No, no, no. I want them all on.' So we took another deep breath ...

What Margaret hadn't told us, though, was that she was having a Cinderella coach – one of those little horse-drawn pumpkin cages that you can just about fit a bride and her dad in. I looked at it. 'Oh my God ...' Now I was the one who felt like crying. There was no way she was going to get into it that with all these underskirts on.

Me and Pauline looked at each other in horror. There was only one thing for it: push. Push. Push. And PUUUUUSH! We literally *squeezed* her into that coach. It was like forcing the icing out of the bag when you're decorating a cake. Finally we got everything stuffed into the coach and Margaret was off to church.

As we watched the horse-drawn carriage trot off, I turned to Pauline: 'You know what, Paul,' I said. 'I can't do this any more.' She looked how I felt. Like I'd just done ten rounds with Mike Tyson. We were shattered.

But it wasn't over yet. Not by a long shot. We had to get Margaret out of the coach at the other end. So we asked some of the other travellers who were milling around their cars for the name of the church, so that we could get there before her, but no one could tell us. We were just standing there saying, 'We don't know what church it is. How's she going to get out of the coach? We need to help her out of the coach.'

We soon discovered another thing about the traveller way of life: they are very, very secretive about the date and time of a wedding. That's one of the main things I've had to learn while working with them. You and me might know where people get married locally and be able to guess it pretty easily, but travellers don't have local places. They get married all over the place, in towns that they don't even know, because they don't live in a settled community.

The main reason they don't say where it is, or when, is because if someone in a town gets wind of the fact that travellers are on their way, often they'll phone the hotel and tell them, and the hotel will probably cancel it.

But they're sometimes also secretive because they don't want certain parts of the families to know where the wedding is, in case there is trouble or a fight. So it's usually just word of mouth on the day. But you can always tell if there's a gypsy wedding happening, because you'll see them driving round, all dressed up, pulling the cars up as they wait for a phone call from someone telling them where it is.

Nowadays I know that if a traveller gives me a date for a wedding, it's not going to be that date. It definitely gives you a rough idea – you know that it will be round about then. But if you phone up the hotel they tell you there'll probably be nothing booked on that date, and all involved will tell you different dates, and it just goes on and on and on like that all the time. It's the way they communicate about everything. Like a secret code. But you get used to it and you start to crack it. I've learned to follow the trails that they leave.

So me and Pauline were having to work all this out for the first time at Margaret's wedding. We just had to jump in a taxi and ask people if they'd seen the Cinderella coach and then try to work out where the wedding was. Eventually we drove up to the right church. Just as we got there we saw six men carrying Margaret towards the door.

That dress weighed over twenty stone. The bride weighed about seven. She couldn't move after they pushed her out of the carriage, so they just picked her up and carried her. God knows how the horse survived!

But there was no doubt that Margaret's dress was really special. It was made entirely of sheeny white Duchess satin, so it was weighty to start with. Then we encrusted it with Swarovski crystals – 20,000 of them because she didn't think that 10,000 was enough. The bodice was also heavy as we had applied a Swarovski zigzag pattern across it. And the skirt was absolutely huge, with a circumference of about forty feet when all the underskirts – layer upon layer upon layer of frothy tulle – were attached. Thank God the train was only twenty feet long. We'd also made her a pair of fingerless gloves that were studded with crystals, and to finish it off we designed a towering Swarovski crown that dazzled away in the sun as she was taken into the church.

I knew how much Margaret wanted her wedding to be in *OK!* magazine and I thought that people would be interested to see it – I mean it's not often you get an unlimited budget and we had really gone for it with this dress. So the day before the wedding I'd called the news desk of the local paper and said: 'I don't know if you're interested, but there's a wedding going on tomorrow in your area. I can't tell you exactly where, but I think the wedding is at such-and-such a hotel. A 16-year-old girl is getting married and she's got a massive big dress. It's covered in crystals and it weighs twenty stone.' The guy at the other end said, 'OK, I'll pass it on.' But he didn't sound that interested.

So we went into the church and watched the wedding. When Margaret came in she got stuck in the aisle, so they had to lift her up and carry her, and then stand her up at the top, next to the groom. That was the first time we'd seen him. He must only have been about 17.

Gypsy girls don't have a huge choice of boys to pick from, as they are only allowed to marry other travellers. That's why they tend to go with boys that they've known all their lives, like a cousin's cousin. They grow up with these lads. Even so, I wasn't sure that I liked the look of Margaret's man, to be honest. I suppose I had begun to feel protective towards her too.

After the wedding there were about five press people, some with huge cameras, outside the church waiting to take a picture of Margaret in the dress. It was like a celebrity wedding. I thought, 'Oh God. What have I done?'

The reporters wanted to speak to Margaret, but she wouldn't go and talk to any of them. They all got their pictures – she was happy to have her photograph taken – but she didn't want to speak.

One of the journalists shouted out: 'Was she late?'

'Yeah, about three hours,' someone shouted back. Me and Pauline laughed, knowing that that was mainly to do with us. But at least her picture made it into one of the tabloid newspapers.

Margaret's wedding brought loads of attention to her and to me. People were talking about it on blogs on the internet, some of them saying how ridiculous the dress was. I suppose lots of people think that about the gypsy dresses, but I think they are missing the point.

What they don't get is that it's all about fantasy. Maybe it goes back to my love of all those historical costumes and old films, but I admire that about the travellers. While most people spend their lives trying to pull back and do what everyone else thinks is the right or nice thing to do, the travellers' attitude is just the opposite. They don't see anything wrong in going over the top. 'Why not make a dream come true?' is their attitude.

So we'd made Margaret's dream come true, and that in turn began to change things for me too. Things really started to take off for me after Margaret's wedding, and I was beginning to become well known. People from all over were calling up the shop asking to talk to 'the gypsy dressmaker'.

When we got back to the hotel for the reception Margaret wanted some of the underskirts off, so we found a big room at the back – a conference room – and started stripping them down. She seemed more comfortable. She could walk, at least. She went off to join the celebrations, but half an hour later she was back. 'Oh, Thelma, I want the skirts back on again. Oh, put them back on.'

Me and Pauline ended up staying in that back room for the rest of the day, taking those bloody skirts off, putting them back on, then off again. Each time it took about an hour. It was exhausting. Even more so because the room was stifling hot and that was making us woozy with exhaustion. Not only that, but all the bridesmaids were coming in and out too. 'Can you loosen this? Will you tighten this bit? Can you make that bit go like that?' It was just a nightmare. 'This is ridiculous,' I kept thinking to myself. But of course traveller weddings were new to me and Pauline then, so we just got on with it.

Someone came in and said, 'Do you want something to eat, girls?' I asked them if we could have it brought to the room. 'I'm not going in there,' I said to Pauline. 'We'll never get a moment's peace and I just need to sit down.'

So we did. There were no seats in the room so we just gathered up some of the tulle underskirts and plonked ourselves down in the middle of a sea of white tulle and ate our dinner off our laps. That moment's peace felt just glorious. And it was a moment, not even a minute, if I recall, because, of course, no sooner had we started to eat our dinner than one of the bridesmaids opened the door. 'Can you just do this?' she said, pointing to her waist. 'Look, I want them back on. Can you put my underskirts back on again?'

Pauline lost it.

'No, we bloody well can't!' she bellowed. 'The whole lot of you can just *go* away! Go on, now, away you go. We're trying to have something to eat here.'

It was about nine o'clock at night. We'd been there for eight hours and had worked the whole time. I don't think many people realise what a physical job it is working on the dresses.

Back then, when they weighed tons, it was especially hard. Taking the skirts off once was tough enough, but doing it for eight hours was torture and the constant 'can you do this, can you do that?', 'I want them on, I want them off', was like added punishment.

Eventually, Pauline looked at me and said, 'Oh my God, Thelma, I'm so tired.'

'So am I. Let's get out of here.'

We couldn't just walk out, though, as the girls would see and call us over to do something. So we asked a couple of the waitresses if there was another way out to the car park that didn't involve us going through the front entrance.

They came back and told us we could go through the kitchen. I phoned a taxi. We still had some of the underskirts that we'd taken off the last time – most of the time we only loan the underskirts – so I was trying to drag these out of the room as quietly as I could.

The kitchen staff were laughing but they helped us get them out. Then we ended up round the back of the place and I could see the taxi. I felt sure we could make it over to the cab quite easily without being spotted. I looked along the wall and could see the wedding guests through the windows.

So I told Pauline to duck below window level and very slowly, with the underskirts in hand, we started to shuffle over to the waiting taxi. But we didn't realise that there were windows on the other side too. As we neared the car, I looked that way and there we saw all the wedding guests standing at the windows watching us. They were all laughing. I think all they could see were the underskirts moving around like some big blancmanges.

We were like, 'Oh shit! That will teach us for trying to be so sly.'

At long last we started to head back to the car. While we were at the wedding we'd managed to get the AA out to fix it, so by about eleven o'clock at night we were finally back in the car on the road to Liverpool. We were so exhausted we couldn't talk, but we'd have plenty to speak about for weeks to come.

8

The Tale of a Not So Happy Ever After

About six months after Margaret's wedding we'd heard that things weren't going well. Someone told us that she and her husband had split up and that he had run off with her best friend. 'Bloody hell, I was right about him,' I thought, when I heard how her young husband had treated her.

They were getting divorced, which I was quite surprised to hear, as divorce is still uncommon in the traveller community. It's not as big a scandal now as it used to be, though, as I do hear of more couples splitting up. When we first started working with travellers the women who came to our shop would be up in arms about any divorcing couples. It was always frowned upon. But then many gypsies are quite religious, so I suppose it's against their beliefs.

However, if a traveller man leaves a marriage, it seems to be OK and less of a shock to the community. For him to run off with whichever girl he wants is accepted. It sounds unfair that traveller women's lives should be controlled by what their husbands want, but I have to say that, from what we hear, most of the couples who get married end up in happy unions. There is, though, no getting away from the fact that gypsy life is male-dominated.

The thing is, the girls know what is expected of them – that their lives will be all about cooking, cleaning and bringing up families – and it's what most traveller girls I've met want to do, because they've never known life any other way. And this is one of the reasons that a lot of gypsy women don't learn to read or write, because they don't need to work. Their job is to keep a good home, and their homes are immaculate. Of course, not all gypsy communities stick so strictly to traditional ways any more, and things are changing – especially with the Romany and English travellers, who are closer to settled people in their thinking than the Irish travellers seem to be.

But still, while most gypsy girls know what lies ahead of them on the domestic front, none of them have been with a man until their wedding day – or, at least, their community forbids it – and so they are not prepared for the relationship side of things. For these girls – and boys – who are so young, it can be a really tough step into married life, especially for the youngsters who end up in abusive relationships.

I know that some of the traveller girls we've worked with live in violent marriages, and I'm aware of at least one couple who have been in that situation for years. But it's still rare for the women to tell me about it. They don't talk about it in their community. Not because they are ashamed of it. It's just that for many travellers, being hit by your husband is not seen as wrong, so it's not worth talking about.

Back in my Paddy's Market days, I could tell the women who were in trouble. I could see their bruises when I was measuring them up and I knew that they were not accidents. You can tell. 'Oh,' I'd say, 'is your fella hurting you?'

'It's all right, it's all right,' would come the reply. 'He's just given me a beating.' These girls brushed it off like it was nothing.

But if a girl we knew was being abused came to do a few fittings with us you could see that she wasn't the same as she had been. Sometimes I could tell just by the fact that there would be a big gap between a girl coming in for a first fitting and the next one. After a few weeks I'd wonder if she was coming back. Then she would eventually, when her marks were fading.

But some of the girls I've worked with do want to talk about it – 'Oh, he's done this,' they'd say – or confide in me about a particular incident.

'Why do you stay? You can get out,' I said to this girl one time. But I didn't understand then. I didn't realise that traveller girls who leave their husbands have nowhere to go. They can't go back to their families, as that brings shame on them, and they only know their own community – traveller girls have no life outside it – so they have to wait a few days for their husband to cool off and then they go back.

I remember this one woman who used to come into Nico not long after we opened. To be honest, you'd find it hard to forget her, as she was so mouthy that we'd ended up having a right set-to in the shop. She had ordered all her bridesmaids' dresses from me, having already bought an off-the-peg wedding dress.

So we did all her bridesmaids' dresses, and then she said she needed an underskirt for her wedding dress. She wanted me to lend her one because she'd spent a lot of money with us. I told her that our underskirts probably wouldn't fit under the dress she'd bought, as it was not made for our skirts. So then she asked if she could borrow a hoop – the frame that goes under the skirts – but ours were all out at the time, so we couldn't lend her anything.

She didn't like this and really kicked off. 'Stick your hoop up your arse,' she screamed and then carried on shouting. Her language was unbelievable. Finally, she left. 'Thank God,' I remember thinking to myself, and hoped that that would be the last of her.

But then she came back a few months later. 'Do you remember the words you said to me when you first came in?' I asked.

'What?' she said.

'You told me stick my hoop up my arse.'

'Oh yeah,' she said. 'Yeah …' and then she looked at me under her eyes and laughed. I started laughing too. She was funny.

We ended up getting on really well that day, and she asked me to make her something special to wear for another wedding she was going to. Her sister was getting married and she wanted a new outfit. So we came up with an idea for a 1940s-style gown that we thought she would like.

She had gorgeous, glossy chestnut-coloured hair and a lovely figure, so over the next few weeks we created her a stunning fitted dress – like something that Veronica Lake would have worn. It was a slinky fit that followed the line of the body, with a corset bodice and a stunning black tulle fishtail hem. But what made it really special was the colour and fabric – a shimmering hot pink dupion silk. She was really tanned as well, so it looked fabulous on her and we even made a little black top hat to match.

When it was finally done she came to Nico to try it on. She looked amazing in it, and we all told her so. She loved it, but there was one thing missing, she said: 'Crystals. Loads of them.' So we got out the Swarovski and showered the whole dress in them. By the time we were finished, it lit up the workshop like a disco ball.

A few weeks later she came back into the shop, but at first we didn't recognise her. She'd obviously been beaten and her face was all puffed up. Her mum was with her and told us what had happened: 'She looked really, really lovely that night in your outfit. Everyone was looking at her,' she said. 'So he put her in hospital. He absolutely battered her.'

Then a few months later she was back, asking us to make another outfit. She'd been quite open about the situation with her man, and we had talked about it, so I said, 'Bloody hell, we'd better not make it too nice or you'll get a beating.' She laughed. 'I will, won't I!'

She's a mum now and has got five kids. She still pops in to see us in the shop from time to time when she's in Liverpool, and we love seeing her. The thing is, you would never, ever imagine a girl like her would put up with that. She is a real character – strong, feisty and funny, and really great company. But then people always find it hard to understand that you don't have to be the shy type to end up in an abusive situation. They look at you as if to say, 'But you're strong, you wouldn't let this happen.' You might be, but it does. And there are loads of reasons why.

I'm definitely no pushover, and I wasn't when I was young either, and yet I ended up married to Kenny, a very controlling man. When I look back and try to work out why I ended up in a situation where someone was dominating me, I keep coming back to the fact that I had really strict parents. I suppose it's taken time to learn that they were strict because they loved me.

Like the gypsy girls, I was very young when I got married. I had just turned 18 and I'd been going out with Kenny for a while. I think that because my mum and dad were so protective, like any young person, I wanted to break free of the rules they laid down. They were far stricter than my friends' mums and dads. I think that's another reason that I understand the young traveller girls – they often want to get married so they can be independent.

I wanted so badly to go out and drink and dance with my friends, but every night I had to be in for nine o'clock and my dad was always waiting for me at the door. So when I met Kenny I was desperate to get away and get married so that I could make my own decisions and do what I wanted.

But I had another reason for wanting to get married. My mum used to do wedding catering and I would help her out. One time we went to this big country house with lovely gardens and I remember thinking, 'What a fantastic place for a wedding. I'd love to get married here.' So I went and found out all the details about it and worked the whole scene out in my head. I wanted a really big wedding. It had to be the best and it was going to be like nothing anyone had ever seen.

Not for me the usual three-tier cake that everybody else had. I ordered a five-tier one. The normal three courses weren't going to be right either – it would have to be five. I was so wrapped up in it all, in the fantasy of it. I suppose that what I was doing was planning my escape into a fantasy life of my own. It had stopped being about the marriage – it was all about the Big Day.

And, just like the gypsy girls, I was always told that good girls don't mess around with boys. 'There's marrying girls and girls who play around,' my mum said to me once. 'If you're one of those and you go with a boy, then no one will ever marry you.'

We did have a special wedding day and my mum made sure that I got everything that I wanted. In fact it was the best wedding day a girl could wish for. What I didn't tell my mum was that, a few weeks before we got married, something had happened between me and Kenny that had left me worried. He used to walk me home at nights – his house was a good hour and a half from mine – and this one night we were walking down a lane and started arguing. I honestly can't remember what it was about, but Kenny got really, really angry. He started screaming and shouting, getting more and more irate. I'd never seen that side of him before and I'd never been so scared.

When I got home I went straight to my room, telling my mum and dad that I was really tired. I had managed to hide the fact that I was upset, but I couldn't sleep that night, thinking about what had happened. I was shocked and shaken, and I started to think that maybe I shouldn't go through with the wedding. How could it have happened? What had I done to make Kenny behave like that? Could I marry someone who made me feel that terrified? Should I?

The next day I knew I had to tell Kenny that everything was over between us, that our relationship was finished and that I didn't want to know. I was devastated. He was really remorseful, saying how sorry he was, that he'd never got that angry before and that he was as shocked as I was. He said that the stress of the wedding was really getting to him and that he was feeling under pressure. He said that when we were married, and it was just the two of us, nothing like that would ever happen again. He kept begging me to go back to him. He didn't know why he did it but he promised it was a one-off and that I wouldn't have to worry about anything like that happening again.

I kept thinking about whether or not to go through with the wedding, but in the end I panicked. 'I've got to marry him now,' I said to myself. 'I've slept with him. Who else would have me? And maybe he's right,' I thought. All the wedding preparations were getting pretty stressful for me too. 'Maybe things will change. Maybe I can change him.'

But of course they didn't, and I couldn't. In the years to come Kenny was mentally abusive time and again when he was drunk. For me that kind of abuse is worse than physical violence – he said such horrible things to me in drink that it constantly chipped away at my sense of self-worth, and over the years Kenny's psychological abuse wore me down and robbed me of my confidence.

Yet, as I said before, on the surface me and Kenny had a perfect life. He had his own business and so did I. We had a

Rolls-Royce. To the outside world we had it all. And my mum and dad thought we did too. It was because my mum was so proud of what we had together – not least our three fantastic kids – that I found it so hard to turn to her when things were breaking down at home.

I remember how she used to speak about one of my relatives who divorced her husband. Everyone in the family was wary of her and called her names. They treated her like she was the devil. Yet all she'd done was leave her husband. But my family was old-fashioned that way and to them she'd committed the worst sin, so she was ostracised. My mum didn't want that to happen to me.

Because of all that, I understand why traveller girls stay and put up with a bad marriage so as not to let their parents down. There was no way I would have left Kenny when I was younger. I thought my mum would never speak to me again if I did and I knew I would bring so much shame on her.

I suppose I'd have to say that for a while at least Kenny was a decent enough husband and father. But as the years went on our home life went from bad to worse. Kenny lived for Fridays, as that was his night in the pub. But he was bad in drink.

Don't get me wrong, I was no angel, but he was very shy without a drink and he didn't like meeting people without having a few first. So, from Saturdays to Thursdays we had a nice family life, but then, come Friday, it was hell.

Friday nights had to be perfect, and I knew that if I wasn't there when he came in, or if I hadn't done the shopping, my life wouldn't be worth living. All week I'd be living on my nerves as Friday got closer. It would be the same scene almost every Friday: Kenny would come back from the pub, drunk, look in the fridge and say, 'There's nothing to eat.'

Now, I made sure that there was a shop in every Friday. 'There is,' I'd say. 'There is.'

'It's all shite,' he'd say, and slam the fridge door.

Then his temper would escalate and he'd accuse me of being no good. He was becoming more and more paranoid and unpredictable. Tracey, my eldest daughter, used to sit through this with me almost every Friday night, watching him get angrier and angrier. It was absolute mental abuse, and because Kenny had a real Jekyll and Hyde personality – something that a lot of abusive people have – we never knew what he was going to come out with next. We all suffered when Kenny's other side took over.

He'd say such horrible things that Tracey would have to try to stick up for me. 'Dad, stop it!' she'd say. Then he'd kick off, shouting at her too.

Some weeks he would be fine, but because I never knew when he was going to kick off I was always tiptoeing about trying to keep the peace, doing anything not to annoy him. But I could guarantee that every Saturday morning it would be the same: he'd be so humble it was unbelievable. He would apologise to me for being so aggressive and say all the usual things about not meaning it and being too drunk.

So Friday may have been his day, but Saturday was mine – and I would give him hell. I knew he wouldn't say anything to me, so on Saturdays I had full control of everything. But it wasn't any way to live, and I walked on eggshells for years.

Tracey and me still talk about those Friday nights, remembering how we used to watch *Prisoner: Cell Block H* on the telly, keeping as quiet as possible, in the hope that he'd fall asleep. Tracey still sees her dad – but I don't think Fridays have ever been our favourite day of the week.

The thing is it's not the money that keeps you in a bad marriage; it's all the trappings of your life – the house, the car – and the security. When you think about getting yourself out of the situation, you constantly think, where will I go? What will I do? How will the kids and me have enough money? These are the things that make it so hard to leave and the reasons that you can't simply get up and walk away.

So, no matter how bad things are at home, I get that it's really, really hard for traveller girls to leave their husbands. I had started to build my own life by the time I left Kenny – I had my own independence. And when we were going through our divorce I was able to get a temporary restraining order against him to stop him 'from using or threatening to use violence' against me. But travellers live in such tight communities that they can't break away from their husbands. And most of them probably wouldn't want to, as it would mean leaving their families behind too. It's hard for outsiders to understand how absolutely impossible these girls' situations can be, but one of the biggest problems is that because they've never worked, and often can't read or write, they don't even have a way to earn money.

I remember a family who used to come to Paddy's in the early days. To be honest, I always thought of them as being a pain in the neck and I didn't much like dealing with them. I thought that they were a bunch of chancers. But I used to feel quite sorry for one of their girls. She was a young, dark girl and she was very, very pretty. She had married this fella who you could see was a bully, and she'd turn up with these bruises on her. You could tell that she was resigned to her lot in life because, beautiful as she was, she looked lifeless.

There was also a younger sister, who was really pretty as well. Now, she'd caused quite a scandal because she'd run away with a lad. Most gypsies are terrified of their girls running away, and that's another reason why they give them everything they want. 'As long as she doesn't let me down, love, as long as she doesn't run off,' is something I've heard a lot when the girls are getting more outrageous with their wedding dress requests.

You see, if a traveller girl runs off with a fella before she's married, that means she's been on her own with a boy, so the family will want to find her and bring her back as quickly as possible. When they do return, the young couple will be kept apart until their wedding can be arranged – that's why some traveller weddings are arranged in such a hurry. Sometimes, though, the boy won't want to marry the girl. He'll bring her back, but she'll be seen as faulty goods. And, after that, no matter how young and pretty she is, it may be that no one wants to marry her. The girl will have to stay with her family for the rest of her life. She's not allowed to work, so she's just kept.

And that is why travellers don't want their girls being with boys before they are married, and why they are chaperoned everywhere. It's also why families are keen to get their girls married as soon as they are old enough.

Family honour also plays a big part. If things start going wrong between a man and a wife, no one will interfere. It's not done. In the same way, if a family's not particularly happy about the fella that a girl has chosen to marry, even if the chances are that he might be a bit handy with his fists, they won't put a stop to it. If they don't let the girl go with him then she might run away, and that's the worst that could happen. It might be breaking their hearts, but they'll let the girls do whatever they want so that they stay at home and don't look to run off. That kid's sister is still not married to this day, and she's really pretty.

One of the things I enjoy most about what I do is talking to the young gypsy girls and listening to their views on all these things. I was having a chat with a young traveller called Bridget when I was in Ireland during the filming of *Big Fat Gypsy Weddings* and it turned into a cracking conversation about relationships.

Bridget was 17 and was getting married. I suppose I wasn't all that surprised by what she thought, but it was the first time I heard similar views from young gypsy girls.

'You know, if your husband comes home and beats you, you must have done something to deserve it,' she said.

'What, even if he's just had a bad day? Or if something's upset him and he comes home and gives you a beating for that? Do you think that's fair, Bridget?' I asked.

'Well,' she said, 'it's a wife's job to comfort her man and to help him through it, to let him see that he's loved.'

I'm looking at her thinking, 'My God, you're 17 and this is what you think; you think that it's a wife's job to be there to help someone who's battering her.'

But the really heartbreaking thing for the gypsy girls in these situations is the fact they've got nowhere else to go. I remember one time, a few years ago, when these two young traveller girls had come to the studio to talk about outfits for a family wedding they were going to. I worked out that they were sisters and could see straight away that the oldest one was quite shy compared to the younger one, who had a real energy about her. They'd been in before, but this time they seemed to hang about the workshop for hours.

Now, I often have to tell my traveller customers that they can only stay in the workshop until a certain hour, as some of them would just sit there all day and gas if I let them. I have a little sofa at the back that's very comfy. It's old and looks a bit Del Boy, and it gets in the way of all the big fabric rolls – we're always pushing it further out the back and I'm sure, if it could, it would roll off of its own accord – but none of us want to get rid of it as it's just so comfortable. I've even slept on it a couple of times, during some all-nighters, so there's no way it's going.

Of course, my customers often get a little too comfy on that old sofa too and, while I like it that they feel at home, it can get a bit much when we're all trying to work. In the end, I said to these girls that we had another customer coming in for a fitting and she didn't want anyone to see the dress so they'd have to leave. So, eventually, off they went.

Later that night, I was the last one still in the workshop as there was a corset that I wasn't very sure about that I couldn't get out of my head, so I wanted to have a closer look when it was quiet. It was starting to get dark and I was thinking about calling it a day. The next thing, I heard a gentle knock at the front door. It startled me a bit, as usually everybody bangs on that door because the buzzer doesn't work and from the front the workshop looks empty, so it's easy to think there's no one there. And though there's a tiny little window to look through, there's a door to the main workshop, so you can't really see anything from out the front. The back door is a corrugated blind. We keep it open all summer and that old sofa even gets a bit of sun some days, as we'll pull it out and sit there having cups of tea. But at night that's all shut up too and from the outside you can't tell anything is going on.

So, after I heard the knock, I walked along the corridor, stopped to ask who was there and then slowly opened the front door. I recognised the younger one's voice. 'Can we come in?' she asked. 'We just want to talk to you about something.'

'OK,' I said, 'what is it, love? What do you want to talk about?' I was busy and I could have done without a chat at that point, but when I looked at them I instinctively knew they needed to come in.

At first they were just talking to me about the upcoming wedding and their outfits, but I had a strong feeling that they didn't really want to go. Then the younger one, who looked about 15, started telling me that her big sister had been getting beaten by her husband. The older girl, who was around 20, was quite beautiful, with long, dark hair. Actually they were both pretty, though the younger one had a feistiness that gave her a cheeky kind of look. It soon transpired that they had run away. The young one who was telling me everything was quite matter-of-fact about it – no tears, nothing – but they were obviously very close and I wondered if it was the young one who had persuaded her older sister to flee.

'We've got nowhere to go,' the young girl told me. 'Can you tell us where to go?'

I knew that they couldn't go back to their own family as it would be seen as shameful on all concerned that they had run away. So I reassured them and said that I'd help find somewhere for them to go in the morning. But for that night I told them they could stay in the workshop with me.

It's just an old industrial unit really, not the relaxing workshop you might imagine a dressmaker to have. I mean, it doesn't have a shower or anything, and that comfy sofa certainly isn't big enough for three. But it's got the basics, and a little kitchen, so I told them to sit down and I made us all some tea and toast.

After that, I carried on working. They seemed happy just chatting away and telling me all about their lives, but no more was said about the reason that they were there. Eventually they fell asleep, both curled up on that old sofa, so I covered them over with some swathes of fabric and went through to my office to try and get some kip in the big chair in there.

The next day I made some calls to find out about refuges and gave them a list of places to try, although I told them they were welcome to come back to our workshop if they needed to. They were so grateful.

I've seen the older sister a few times since then, but she never did stay the night again. It seems like her home life has settled down a bit as well – she and her husband look much happier and they've got quite a few kids now.

Sometimes all the traveller girls need are a few days away, because in the end they know they have to go back. What else can they do? Their community is the only thing they know. And, because of how isolated traveller communities are, it can be hard for anyone else to know what's going on, or for the girls to speak out. Often they have no one to talk to.

Some abused traveller women won't look for help because they worry that they might not be welcome in places outside their world. It's a problem that campaigners have highlighted over the past couple of years, and there are now refuges aimed specifically at traveller girls. So, if a woman needs to get away from a violent partner or a husband who has been binge drinking, she can spend a couple of weeks at one of these places while the situation at home calms down.

One of our regular customers is always in and out of a refuge. And there was another girl who came to pick a dress up once who'd just come out of one. She was meant to come at a certain time but didn't turn up – which is not unusual, as gypsies often seem to do things in their own time. But there was something about this girl that time that made me worry. We were locking up for the night, so I phoned her to let her know. But she didn't pick up – her husband did. 'She's not here, love,' he said.

'Oh, she's supposed to be picking this outfit up,' I told him, 'and I don't know what to do – whether to go or to stay or what. Have you any idea when she might be coming for it?'

'Oh, I don't know,' he said. 'We had a little bit of an argument, so when she gets there will you tell her to phone me?'

'Yeah, OK,' I said.

Then she turned up. 'My God. What's happened to your lip?' I said, not thinking. Her lip was all big and puffy and stitched up with butterfly stitches. She told me she'd been out for three days because her husband had beaten her.

'Bloody hell, I've just phoned your husband,' I said, apologetically. 'He wants you to phone him.'

'I'm not phoning him,' she said.

'But you're going to go back?' I asked her.

'Well, yeah,' she said, 'and I'm still going to the wedding as well, so have you got the outfits?'

When we highlighted some cases of domestic abuse in an episode of *Big Fat Gypsy Weddings*, I had a call from a Romany girl who wanted to question why we had shown it, as she thought it made it seem like domestic abuse is a big part of gypsy life.

'Our girls won't be pushed around,' she shouted at me down the phone. 'We're not all subjects of domestic violence, you know. Don't make out that it's all of us. We don't all do that!'

Of course, she's right. I think traveller culture is like any other in that respect – some fellas are good, some are bad.

9

The Tale of the Unpaid Bill

Now, while a few gypsy girls might end up with not-so-good fellas, the one man that a traveller girl can always depend on, especially when it comes to her Big Day, is her dad. Often, when a girl comes to us to have a dress made, it's her dad, as the head of the family and the one in charge of the finances, who will start the ball rolling by calling me up first. Basically, he's calling to let me know that whatever his daughter wants he will pay for it, and that the deposit is on its way. After that we tend to deal with the mum.

I remember this one Irish traveller who phoned me up and asked us if we could make his daughter's wedding dress. They lived in southern Ireland and couldn't come to Liverpool, so he asked if we could meet with his daughter and wife while we were over there doing another wedding, and said he'd give them the deposit to pass on.

So we agreed to meet them in Dublin on our way back to Liverpool, so that we could measure up the girl and get the order sorted to start on when we got back. We got the mum on the phone and said we'd meet her in this café at a certain time. We waited for her and her daughter to arrive. Finally they turned up – but as well as her daughter she had about twenty other family members in tow. It was pandemonium, but it was also quite funny and, as always, unpredictable.

We talked about the dress and the mum said that she had the deposit. Only she'd brought a cheque, and it was an Irish cheque, made out in euros. 'We don't take euros,' I told her. But she didn't have anything else, so I said I'd take the cheque but that when she came to pay the rest of the money and collect the dress she'd have to pay in pounds. So we sketched out the dress her daughter wanted, measured the girl and told her we'd see them in Liverpool when the dress was ready.

A few months later the family came over to Liverpool to pick up the dress. The dad was with them this time, and he seemed like a nice enough fella. So it came to paying and he asked me to knock something off and the haggling started. But I was used to that, so I took some money off. Then he wanted me to knock more off. It kept on like this, and he was saying, 'Oh, come on, I've got another daughter.' But all my customers say that – 'I've got another four daughters' – hoping that offering me the chance to make all their girls' dresses as a job lot will get them more discount.

So this fella was like, 'Yeah, yeah, yeah, OK,' and he stopped haggling. But they love all the banter – and travellers are great at it. That's another reason that I like working with them, they're funny. And he was a good laugh, this fella.

We said we'd have everything ready for them to come back and pick up at two o'clock. We fitted the dress on the girl. She looked really lovely and the whole family was delighted. So the girls in the workshop started to undress the bride-to-be and pack everything up ready for the family to take back to Ireland, Pauline took the father into the back office to settle the bill, and I went into the front office to have a business meeting with a couple of guys who had just arrived.

A couple of minutes later Pauline popped her head around the door: 'Sorry to bother you, Thelma, but can you come through? The dad wants to see you.'

I told the two fellas that I'd be back in a minute and followed Pauline down the corridor. 'What's up?' I asked her.

'He wants to pay in euros,' Pauline told me. 'I told him we don't take euros, but he's not having it from me, so he wants to see you.'

I walked into the office and smiled at the dad. 'Sorry, you can't pay in euros.'

'Why, love?' he asked.

'Because it's England and we don't take euros,' I told him.

I could tell he was getting really annoyed, as his voice started getting louder and louder as he carried on arguing with me.

'All you have to do is go to the bank and change the money into sterling,' I said. 'Problem solved.' I had to get back to the meeting, so I left him with Pauline, who said she'd find out where the nearest branch was.

A minute or two later I could hear all this shouting going on and Pauline was at the door again. 'I think you'd better come through, Thelma,' she said. 'He's going berserk, banging on the table and punching the door.'

Pauline was fuming as we went back through. 'He's still saying he wants to pay in euros,' she said.

'Well, he can't pay in euros. I've told him that,' I said looking at her, then at him.

'What's your problem?' I asked. 'Can you go to France and pay in pounds? No, you can't,' I told him, before he got a chance to answer. 'You've got to pay in the currency of whatever country you're in.'

'No! No! I've brought euros,' he shouted back.

'I don't care what you've brought, we don't take euros,' I said.

'Well, you can keep your dress and give me my deposit back,' he said.

'No, I'm not giving you your deposit back,' I said. 'We took that to make the dress.'

THE COMMUNION SEASON GETS GOING:
(Clockwise from top left) A young traveller in dress and crown at her First Communion, with her little sister, also dressed for the occasion; a Communion dress with a ballroom twist; a young Irish traveller arrives at her First Communion in a pink limo; a twinkling top hat adds Hollywood style to this Communion outfit; a sunny smile in a sunflower Communion dress.

**Teen bride Car[...]
Jordan. So she[...]
dress made tha[...]**

RIDEGROOM [...]
glanced nervou[...]
he waited at th[...]
had gone to pla[...]
would by now [...]
vows with his 16-year-[...]
Carly O'Brien. But she[...]
late. Had she changed [...]

The truth was much [...]
Carly didn't have a bad [...]
jitters, she was actually [...]
by more pressing matte[...]

In a bid to oversh[...]
and Peter Andre[...]
wedding, she [...]
£15,000 w[...]
1,600m [...]
120m [...]
with [...]
C[...]
26[...]
k[...]
w[...]

J[...]
st[...]
a t[...]
hel[...]
took [...]
hours [...]

CINDERELLA FOR A DAY: When Katie Price arrived for her wedding in 2005 in a Cinderella pumpkin coach, she started a trend – it's now the most popular means of transport for young traveller brides.

HER CARRIAGE AWAITS: This young traveller arrived at her First Communion in a Cinderella coach. Her dad shipped it all the way from America. It's the same coach all the traveller brides use to this day and the one that Katie Price used as well.

TWO IN ONE: This mini-skirt was worn by the bride at her evening celebration. Unusually for a traveller bride, this girl didn't want to wear her heavy wedding skirts all night.

A CHRISTMAS GYPSY WEDDING: Charleen is held up by her daddy on the way to the church. Mind you, with that skirt on, I am sure she would bounce right back up if she slipped! We used a mile of fabric to make this dress.

TWISTS AND TURNS: Melissa wanted a curling 30-foot train. In the end it was too long to be stretched out in our shop.

GREAT EXPECTATIONS: Vanessa, from Rathkeale, was only a tiny little thing, but she still insisted on one of the biggest dresses we've ever made.

THREE HEADS, ONE DRESS: Me and Pauline giving one of our brides the finishing touches. Believe it or not, there's a girl under there!

IT'S ALL IN THE DETAIL: Leanne always models our new designs to check they sit perfectly and achieve the exact look we want.

CHERRY BLOSSOM: All of our traveller customers want their wedding dresses to be completely original. Lavinia's was covered in diamanté cherries. Despite her husband-to-be keeping her waiting for hours on the big day, she looked beautiful and had a wonderful time.

FAN-TASTIC: Inspired by the structural designs of my fashion idol Alexander McQueen, this was the first wedding dress we made that didn't have a single crystal on it.

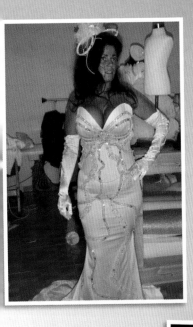

DREAMS FROM THE BIG SCREEN: Our young traveller brides are often inspired by the fairytale dresses they see in Disney films. This bride's dress (right) was based on *The Princess and the Frog*. The bodice alone weighed over 20 pounds. The groom refused to wear the prince's suit, so the bride made her younger brother (top right) wear it instead. The mother of the bride (top left) based her outfit on Cheryl Cole's wedding dress.

STAR TURN: (Top) At the 2011 BAFTAs with the lovely Sheridan Smith, star of *Two Pints of Lager and a Packet of Crisps*. (Bottom) In January last year I was a guest on *Alan Carr: Chatty Man*. Here I am in the green room with the man himself after we finished filming.

'Well, keep the deposit, and keep your dress, right,' he snapped. And then he pointed at his wife, who had been standing there with their daughter the whole time. 'And you can keep her as well.'

'So, what you want is for me to take your dress and your wife,' I said.

'Yeah!' he said.

So then, of course, the daughter starts screaming, 'No, Daddy. No. I want my dress. I want my dress.'

Honestly, it was hysterical, but he wasn't laughing, he was proper red-faced angry and you could tell he just wanted to hit someone.

'Do you know what?' I said. 'You're acting like a big bully and I'm telling you, just because you shout louder it doesn't mean you're going to get heard, and until you calm down I am not going to talk to you, so either get out and calm yourself down or go home. Whichever way you want to do it, it's fine with me.'

So he stormed out of the room. Meanwhile, the mother just rolls her eyes and the daughter's calmed down and is now just talking to me like normal, pointing at the dress, saying, 'Can I have such-and-such a thing on it? And can I have this?' Everyone at the other end of the workshop was standing there with their mouths wide open.

I thought for a moment. 'I'll be back in a minute,' I said, and went off to call the bank to find out what the exchange rate would be. When I got back, he was back with the mother and daughter. So I told him what the rate was and how many euros it would be. But he wouldn't have that either, so then we were there for another hour, arguing about the exchange rate.

'No,' I kept telling him, when he tried to beat me down on the euro figure. 'That's what it's going to cost and I'm not accepting any less!' Then there was more arguing, more going on about paying in euros, more going on about taking the dress, about not taking the dress – the whole kerfuffle lasted about two hours.

Pauline put a stop to it all in the end. '*You know what*,' she screamed, banging her fist on desk, 'I'm getting a headache! *And I don't get headaches!*' I just burst out laughing at that point and everyone else in the workshop did too.

The next thing, the dad gets up, gives me the amount of euros I asked for in the first place, holds out his hand and says to me, 'Nice doing business with you.' I looked at him in utter disbelief. Then he said, 'And will you do my other daughter an outfit? It'll be sterling, then. I'll pay you in sterling.' I just looked at him.

'Oh, it's all good craic, love. It's all good craic,' he said, smiling.

'Yeah, OK, brilliant,' I said. And off he went.

Pauline and I just looked at each other in utter disbelief. 'What about the guys in the office?' asked Pauline.

'Oh God, I forgot all about them,' I said. Pauline came back to the office with me and said hello as if it was business as usual, which, in a way, it was for us.

'Did you see their faces?' Pauline asked me when we were locking up that night. 'I think they were in shock.' We just looked at each other and laughed, knowing that, to the outside world, ours was unbelievable.

When I started, the travellers' tendency to flare up like that did kind of frighten me, but I'm used to dealing with it on the spot now because I know it's all about the drama. I've learned that their bark is far, far worse than their bite. Which means that I often feel a bit like a teacher in charge of a classroom of petulant children.

I can see them thinking, 'I'll stamp my feet, I'll kick the wall, and I'll scream and shout so loud that I'll get what I want.' But my attitude to that kind of tactic is the same as it is with my own kids: crying doesn't get you what you want.

The thing is, my gypsy customers all think they're the first ones to blow up at me and that I'll be so shocked that I'll give them what they want, but we've handled so many unpredictable scenarios now that we're pretty used to it, so that kind of dramatic behaviour just doesn't cut it with us.

I was telling a friend all about this one day, and she looked at me and said, 'Yeah, the travellers sound like a good laugh, unless they're living next door to you. They are all nuts. How can you bear working with them?'

'They're just different to us,' I said. 'They're used to living in their own world.'

I know that a lot of people won't work with travellers because of the fact they can be aggressive and shout and be generally noisy, but it's just the way they communicate. It's all about the drama. They love drama.

It works the other way too. My gypsy customers are, on the whole, charming to work with. In my experience they are lovely, funny people, and all this kicking off that they do is mostly a con; it's just their way. They are very respectful of me and they tell each other, 'She's a nice woman. Don't muck her around.'

They are also very loyal. I heard about one of our regular traveller customers blowing her top at someone in Ireland who was trying to do us down. Then there was the time, after the TV show had been a hit, when one of the tabloids did a story about the fact that I had been sent to jail.

The headline said something like 'Big Fat Gypsy Liar'. I knew it would happen at some point and I've always been open with everyone about my time in prison – I have never tried to hide it, and the people I love and who love me know about it anyway. I had also told the television production company about it before we started filming. Still, it wasn't very nice for any of us to see it splashed all over the papers all these years later.

The story came out on a Saturday morning, and by eleven o'clock that day Paddy Doherty – the *Celebrity Big Brother* winner – had come to the factory and was shouting, 'Who do they think they are, writing that about you? You're in my heart, and if anyone hurts you they hurt me.'

'Look, Paddy,' I replied, 'what can I say? I knew it was going to come out, and there's nothing I can do about all of that.'

'I'm telling you now,' he said. 'If anyone ever comes in here causing trouble, I am twenty minutes away. Get on the phone to me and I'll be here to sort it out.' His support for me that day meant a lot.

When I first started working with the travelling communities I had no idea how prejudiced people were against them. But I remember the first time I experienced it. We'd met this family and got on really well with the dad, Larry, who had bought his first daughter's wedding dress from me. I was now making a dress for his second daughter, who was about to get married. The day that Larry turned up to pay the deposit, he said out of the blue, 'Can you do us a favour? Can you ring this hotel and see if you can book me a room for the wedding date?'

At first I thought he was just being dead cheeky, so I said, 'Do it yourself!'

'Oh, go on; go on, will you do it for me? Do it for me, go on.' He went on and on like that, and so, just to shut him up, I said I'd do it. I still didn't understand why he was asking me, but I got on the phone to the hotel and tried to book the wedding rooms.

I told the receptionist what I wanted and she told me that they had four reception rooms available and asked me if I wanted to come down and see them so that I could choose the one I wanted, and we could go through menus and things.

'Brilliant,' I said, 'thanks very much,' and put down the phone. So Larry came back later that day and I told him that it was all sorted and that all he had to do was to go down and pick the room and put a deposit down.

He went to the hotel a couple of days later, and then came back to see me. 'Which room did you pick?' I asked him. 'What did you think?' But he told me that when he got there they told him that the hotel was all fully booked for that day.

I was really surprised. It didn't make sense. I felt a bit stupid, thinking I must have picked it all up wrong. 'They told me that all the rooms were available,' I said to him. 'That's weird.'

So I said I'd call them back to see what was going on. When I got someone on the line I explained that I'd called up a few days before asking about wedding rooms and the girl had said to come down and have a look. 'The gentleman came down to pick a room,' I said, 'but someone told him that the hotel was all booked up that day. Has there been a mistake?' I asked.

'Hold on a minute,' she said, as she went to talk to her manager. She came back and told me, 'Oh, the girl who was on the desk at the time didn't realise that we had a convention booked that's going to take over the whole hotel that day.'

'Oh, right. OK,' I said, while I thought, 'If she worked for me, I'd sack that girl for being so stupid.' But then I went over it all again in my mind and I knew that something wasn't right. So I decided to go down to the hotel myself. When I got there I chatted to the girl on the desk and told her that I wanted to book the function room for that date.

She said the date was fine and then asked me if I'd like to have a look around. 'Oh my God,' I thought, 'this is unbelievable.' I just looked at her and said, 'I can't believe this.'

She looked puzzled. 'Sorry?'

'I actually phoned up to book the hotel and was told it was available, yet when the gentleman came down to view it he was told it wasn't available. Now you're telling me it is available again.'

'Oh, I think there have been crossed wires,' she said.

'No, there are no crossed wires,' I said. 'What's the problem? I'm not going to leave this.'

She told me her manager wasn't there but that she'd get him to call me. I was so furious that I called myself as soon as I got to the workshop and got put through to him. I explained everything to him and he was very frank. 'What it is,' he said, 'is that these people are travellers.'

'Yeah?' I said.

'We've had trouble with travellers before,' he told me, 'and we can't really accommodate them.'

'You've had trouble with Larry, the man who came to look at the room?' I asked him.

'No, not him, but we've had trouble with other travellers,' he said.

'That's a racist statement you've just made there – you do realise that?' I replied.

'Not really,' he said.

That's what he said. 'Not really.' I couldn't believe that he thought it was OK to say that, that it was OK for him to tar everyone with the same brush.

Now, I've been to the weddings of settled people where there have been big fights, and I've been to weddings where there hasn't been a fight, and I've been to a posh wedding where there's been a hell of a fight! I've done thousands of traveller weddings now, thousands of them, and there's not always a fight. And the big difference is that if a fight kicks off at a traveller wedding it finishes almost as soon as it starts, because all the elders are there and they don't let it get out of control. There's always someone like Paddy Doherty there to stop it.

Not all travellers are the same, in the same way that not all other ethnic groups are. I think people often don't even realise that there are different types of gypsies: English, Irish and

Romany. They all do things differently and we work with them all.

The Romanies see themselves as being the most deserving of the word 'gypsy', because their history goes back much further than the other communities. It's quite ironic that the Romany and English travellers are a bit more up to date in their ways. The Irish travellers have the most recent history, yet they tend to be far more traditional.

Most Romany girls finish school and want to go out and get jobs, even though they will probably give their job up when they get married. But then they usually get married in their early 20s, unlike the Irish girls, who normally get married very young and generally don't finish school.

It's an accepted thing that many Irish travellers can't read and write. Sometimes they'll come into the workshop, and if I happen to point at something in the paper and say, 'Oh, look at that,' they'll reply, 'What does it say?' The new generation is into texting, though, so that's sort of taught them how to write. Mind you, working out what they've written is another story, and I often have to look at a text for about half an hour before I understand it.

Some of the Romanies can be really awful about the Irish gypsies. A Romany girl called me once to ask me to do a wedding dress for her. We were having a normal chat and she was giving me the usual, 'I want it bigger and better, and …' And then she carried on, 'I want it better than that dog that was on the TV because I'm a true Romany and she's not.' She was being really derogatory about the Irish travellers, so I put the phone down on her.

You see, some of the Romanies were unhappy about the way travellers were portrayed in *Big Fat Gypsy Weddings*, and they hate the idea that everyone thinks all gypsies are the same. I had a couple of phone calls from Romany girls after some of the first programmes went out. They were up in arms about the way gypsies were being portrayed. 'Our girls won't be pushed around, you know,' one of them said to me. 'We're not all subjects of domestic violence. We work, we do this, we do that.'

They really thought it was my fault and that, by being on the programme, I had let them down in some way. I was a bit shocked. One of them said, 'We're gypsies. We put you where you are. I bought off you in the market …' I told her that I have never denied that it was the travellers who put my business where it is today – gypsies are my business. But I also let her know that I have never, ever knocked travellers of any kind. I wouldn't take part in anything that did that and, in fact, I turned down the chance to be in TV programmes for years before *Big Fat Gypsy Weddings* for that very reason.

Another Romany girl called me up and said, 'Who do you think you are, portraying us like that, like the Irish?' I just let her go on, and then told her that the series had only just started, and that if she watched it right through to the end she'd see Romany and English travellers' ways, too. 'Are you a traveller?' she asked. 'Are you ashamed of being a traveller? Are you ashamed of it?' I told her I wasn't a traveller and managed to calm her down. 'Wait until the end of the series and see what you think,' I said. 'Phone me back then. In fact, give me your number, and I'll phone *you* back.' And I did. I was on the phone to her for about an hour that time, and in the end she was talking to me as though I was her best friend.

Another time, two Romany girls came up to me. 'I go to school,' one of them said, 'and she goes to college,' pointing at her mate. 'And I earn my own money and I do this and I do that.' Again, I told her that we weren't trying to say that all travellers are the same, and that I wasn't trying to be the authority on traveller life. 'We just talk about what happens when we do the weddings,' I told her. 'I'm not trying to say this, that or the next thing.' Then she asked if she could come and work for me! I'll say this for them – Romany girls are nothing if not feisty.

And yet, not all the Romanies were up in arms about *Big Fat Gypsy Weddings*. In fact, Billy Welch, a leading member and spokesperson of the traveller community, said that he liked the show because it opened people's eyes to the kind of prejudice travellers face.

And Irish travellers will often stop me in the street and shake my hand, or send me Facebook messages saying 'Thanks for sticking up for us.'

Only recently, I was talking to a young Irish traveller girl who felt that the Romanies look down on them. 'They say we're dirty and we're this and we're that,' she said. 'It wasn't that long ago they were sitting round a fire with a wooden spoon, you know.' So, like any society, the gypsies also have their own prejudices, and the Irish and the Romanies are absolutely not the same.

Now I find it easy to tell which gypsy faction the girls come from. You can usually spot it by the way they dress. The Irish travellers generally like quite revealing outfits, like short skirts and high boots with diamanté all over them, and have something of an in-your-face style, whereas the Romanies aren't like that at all, preferring outfits that cover them up a bit more.

Travellers have different tastes in how they like to dress their kids too. My Romany customers love the little smock dresses that I used to make at Paddy's – the sticky-out ones, like the first *Gone With the Wind* dresses I made. They just love anything Victorian-looking. The Irish travellers, on the other hand, like the more blingy, diamanté-sprinkled things.

Irish gypsy weddings are the most flamboyant ones too. Romany and English ones are more like non-traveller weddings. They still stick to the basic traveller wedding traditions, such as not sending out invitations and so on, but their weddings are less chaotic and unpredictable than those of the Irish travellers.

The fact is, there are always exceptions. And travellers in general are exceptions to every rule. It's just the way they are. I don't understand why so many people feel that travellers should be made to conform and settle down, so that they fit into the society of settled communities. While I wouldn't say I like everything about the way travellers live, I sometimes wonder if non-travellers might not learn from them and get back some of the things that society has lost.

Lots of travellers think that the morals of some people in settled communities are disgusting. The idea that girls can go out with boys before they are married, or go out and get blind drunk with their mates on a Friday night, is shocking to them. They are very protective of their kids and don't want them out having sex or doing drugs at the age of 14. The gypsies disapprove of the idea of there being no restrictions, no rules and everyone just doing what they like.

Many might argue that gypsies have no respect for the way of life of those in settled communities, but I honestly don't think the travellers are being deliberately disrespectful. I think it's just their tradition to live life the way they are used to.

10

The Tale of the Girl Who Dreamed of Being a 'Swan Pumpkin'

Now, travellers also stick to their ways when it comes to telling me what their budget for a dress is. Most of the girls will say the same thing: 'The sky's the limit.' It sounds fantastic, and it is – so much so that you really need to have someone like Pauline on hand, who is not afraid to say, 'No, that's it now, that's enough,' to bring everyone back down to earth.

The more outrageous the request, the longer a dress takes to create and the more expensive it will be. Lucky for me, with Pauline keeping an eye on the practical side of things, I can get on with the job of bringing the girls' fantasy wedding dresses to life.

When a traveller girl comes in to see us for the first time to discuss the dress that she wants us to make, naturally she will be really excited and overflowing with a wish-list of ideas. Their wedding day is their big chance to be a princess for a day, just like the girls they see in Disney films, and these girls just love anything to do with Disney – I've even done a dress like the Little Mermaid, with a fishtail skirt stitched to look like it was made of scales that came down into a point.

Movies are a big influence on traveller girls, and that's where they get a lot of their dress ideas from. We are always being handed DVDs of films, especially the ones that have big wedding scenes in them. The most popular of all is *Coming to America*, the 1980s film where Shari Headley comes down the aisle in a massive pink dress and marries Eddie Murphy's character, the African prince. They all just adore that film.

They also love pop stars like Beyoncé and Shakira, but they are not so into British celebrities like Cheryl Cole and Victoria Beckham. I think they really love the dancing and the glitzy clothes the American stars wear.

But while some of the girls want their dresses to look just like the ones they see on the screen, others have very individual ideas about what they want. One of the first really outrageous designs I was asked to make was for another girl called Margaret, who came into Nico not long after we opened. We'd made her sister's dress a while before, and now it was her turn to be the bride.

'I want a swan,' she said.

'OK,' I said. 'Do you want the swan on the front, stitched on?

'No,' she said, 'I want it so that it looks as though I am coming out of the swan, like I am inside it. I want one side of the swan on the front and the other side of the swan on the back, so that the wing goes up my side, all covered in feathers made out of Swarovski crystals. And then I want the neck of the swan to twist around my neck, so that its head falls down the front.'

The reason she chose a swan, she told me, was that she'd heard that swans mate for life.

I was sketching all this out as she was talking to me.

'Oh, and I don't want an ordinary skirt,' she said.

'Right,' I said.

'I want a pumpkin.'

'A pumpkin?' I said, and looked at her.

'Yeah,' she replied. 'I want it to be a pumpkin on the bottom and a swan on top.'

'OK,' I said. 'We can do that for you, no problem.'

And we did.

The swan was easy. The pumpkin was a bloody nightmare!

The skirt was huge and we had to gather it underneath to make the pumpkin shape, so that the girl could walk in it without tripping up. In the end I had to think back to my early days, when I made that first dress for Mary's daughter and had to devise a way to make the 107-foot train work. Just like we did then, we had to make a special frame to allow the pumpkin skirt to move when the bride walked.

That was another one of our dresses that made the news. The bride was interviewed for Granada's *North West Tonight* programme. She looked really lovely in it, surrounded by all her bridesmaids, and she told the story about swans mating for life. They asked her if the dress was heavy. 'Yeah, it's already killing me,' she said, 'and I've got to wear it until about twelve o'clock tonight.'

The girls often get quite bruised wearing such heavy dresses for the whole day, but some of them see their bruises as a badge of honour – I've known girls ask us to make their dress heavier than another girl's to make sure they can show off the marks. I also know that a few of the girls wear these wheelie trainers under their dresses, just so they can move. That's not as easy as it sounds, though, because to get the shoes to stop and start, you've got to control them, like the clutch on a car, and it can take a bit of getting used to.

A year or so ago, we were at a wedding where the bride just couldn't get the hang of these wheelie shoes. Her dress was really heavy, more like the ones we made in the early days. We don't make so many of these now, but she was dead keen for us to make it weigh as much as we – and she – could get away with. But every time she tried to kick-start the trainers she stalled. It was dead funny, because she would stop so suddenly that her body would wobble back and forward and she'd be rocking around like something from a pantomime.

In the end someone had to go off and get two fellas to pull her forward and wheel her towards the altar. Then when the wedding was finished they had to turn her around and push her back out. When we got back to the wedding reception she was determined to keep all the skirts and the trainers on. But she still couldn't work them, so she just sat and had her meal and didn't leave the table for the rest of the night. She had no choice – she couldn't move. But she was happy.

You see, nothing will stop these girls living their dream for a day. And that's why we will never say no to anything they want. We might have to modify things to make them work, but we never say no. And, do you know, nothing they ask for even shocks me any more.

But I'll never forget this one bride who came in and said that she wanted a tiger's head on the bodice of her dress – a tiger with a big open mouth. 'Yeah, OK, we'll do a tiger's head for you, no problem,' I said.

'Shall we put something in its mouth?' I asked, 'like it's just killed something and the blood is coming down the dress in red diamonds?' I said it for fun, but she liked the idea and I actually ended up having to talk her out of it.

'I'm only joking!' I laughed. 'Of course, you can have whatever you want, but I think that a tiger with something dead hanging out of its mouth might not look very good.'

'Oh, what's wrong with that?' she asked.

'Well, I just don't think the red diamonds on the white will look that nice,' I said.

Then there was this other girl who came in and said, 'I want something that no one's ever had before. I want a dress with Baby Phat on it.'

'Baby Phat – as in the actual brand?' I asked her.

'Yeah,' she said. 'And I want the whole front of the corset to be that Baby Phat cat.'

She wanted the cat's tail to go around the back of the dress and then down her neck, like the swan dress we'd done. Then she came back and said she wanted Baby Phat cats made out of Swarovski crystals on the dress, facing each other so the cats' tails curled up to make a heart shape. One on each side and one on the back. She also asked for a Baby Phat necklace, bracelet and earrings, and she even wanted us to write 'BABY PHAT' in crystals along the bottom of the dress.

A few of the girls like to have things written in crystals on their dress. One asked us to write 'SWAROVSKI' on hers, but someone told us that we might have problems with the brand copyright if we did that, so we told her we probably couldn't. But she was adamant, so I said that the only thing we could do was spell it differently. 'It doesn't matter how you spell it,' she said to me, 'as long as it says Swarovski.' So we just did an 'o' instead of the 'a' and stitched 'SWOROVSKI' on the dress.

When we put that dress up on Facebook someone sent us a message saying, 'I can't believe you spelt that wrong. I can't believe you're charging all that money to let a bride walk down the aisle with that spelt wrong on her dress.'

I didn't reply, but one of our fans did: 'She's a dressmaker not an English teacher!' she wrote. We got about 300 comments on that post – it went on for ages, everyone arguing about the way it was spelt.

Another girl, Melissa, wanted the names of her and her husband written in Swarovski crystals on the train of her dress, inside a crystal love heart. But when she came to pick the dress up she just stood, staring at it. 'Who's Patrick?' she asked, looking up at all of us who were gathered round waiting for her to try it on.

'Your husband-to-be,' I said, looking at her with surprise.

'No, the fella I'm marrying is called Joe,' she said.

'Oh no,' I said, realising that the wires had got crossed somewhere.

'Oh, it's fine,' she said. 'He can't read.'

I was mortified – there was no way I could let her wear it. 'Well, you'll just have to do without the train,' I said. 'We don't have time to make another one and you can't walk down the aisle with the wrong fella's name on it!'

'Oh, no. Oh, no, you can't do that,' she said. 'I can't not have the train. Please just leave it, Thelma, please. It doesn't matter. He won't notice, honestly.'

I could see she was devastated with the idea of not having a train, but there's no way I was going to let her do that, regardless of who could or couldn't read it. We had all liked working with this girl, so we agreed among ourselves to do an all-nighter – unpicking the name and then sewing the right one on – so that the train, with 'JOE' sparkling along the edge in Swarovski, would be ready in time for the wedding the next day.

Although in one way the travellers can be difficult customers, in another they're really easy, because they don't complain about little things and they are usually happy to give us *carte blanche* with the designs, as long as the basic big shape is there. We do get the odd English bride, or local Liverpool girl, looking for us to make their dresses, and they tend to come in and be picky about everything. They'll try the dress on and everything is OK, and then in the final fitting they'll find the tiniest mark, or something else won't be quite right. But you don't get that with travellers. They just don't do that finicky thing. All of our customers know now that we know what they want, so they are happy just to let us get on with it.

Of course, the only way I can make all these amazing requests come true is because of all the girls in the workshop. There's Pauline, who's been with me forever, and is in charge of the shop. She does much more than that, though – she's my rock.

And she's the only person I know who still gets butterflies in her stomach every time we finish a dress.

Then there's Yanli, who's now the corset-maker. The corsets are really what give our business legs, and it's important that someone is always being trained in the way we make them, as it's a highly skilled job. These days Yanli always has a trainee corset-maker working with her, so if she is off ill someone else can take over. It's unlikely that any of them will be as good as her, but as long as they know the basics we can finish them.

Then we've got Stacey, the head machinist. She is in charge of the sewing room and does all the underskirts and the big wedding-dress skirts, all the basics. Stacey's a real character, and I'll never forget the day that she first rang the bell at Nico.

I opened the door and she said, 'Me want job.'

'Sorry?' I said, looking at her.

'Job. Me,' she said.

I had an auntie who was deaf and dumb, and the way this woman spoke made me think that she might be deaf too.

'Can you sew?' I asked her in sign language – I was taught sign language as a child by my Aunty Joan. 'You go home and sew something and bring it back to show me,' I said.

She just looked at me and started dialling on her mobile phone. She moved out of earshot to speak to someone and then handed the phone to me. 'Hello, this is Stacey's sister,' came the voice at the other end of the line.

'Hi,' I said. 'Will you just explain to her to sew something and bring it back to me so that I can have a look at what she can do?' My sign language was obviously a bit rusty.

'She's got something with her to show you,' her sister said.

So I'm looking at her and trying to sign slowly that I want her to show me what she's got. I wasn't really getting anywhere, but eventually she pulled a pair of trousers out and showed them to me. 'Bloody hell,' I said to myself, as I looked them over. They were amazing – well cut, well sewn, everything about them was perfect. The hemming, the buttonholes, everything.

'OK,' I said to her, as though I was deaf and dumb too. 'Trousers. Are. Very. Good. You. Come. Monday. I give you one month trial.' I did think it was a bit odd that she had just turned up on the doorstep, but I knew she was good. And seamstresses like Stacey don't come along very often.

So Stacey came back to start working with us the following week and I found out that she wasn't deaf and dumb after all – she was from Lithuania and just talked a bit funny. She was a little bit odd, though, and I started to wonder whether she'd been planted by the DSS. I've always made sure that I do everything by the book after what happened before and going to prison, but I was still a bit nervy. But then Stacey's English was so bad that I reckoned that there was no way she could have worked for anybody. And her employee information was all completely legal, so it was just me being a little over-anxious.

'Why did you come in to see me?' I asked her one day. She just looked at me, repeating 'Why? Why?' over and over. 'Oh Jesus,' I thought and went to get a dictionary to show her so that she could start learning new words.

And that's how I started helping Stacey with her English. She was going to college to learn, but I gave her the dictionary and showed her new words every day. Then I'd tell her to take it home and look at it at night and work some things out, and every morning she would come in and say, with a big smile, 'Understand now.'

When I got to know her better, I told her, 'I thought you were deaf and dumb when you first turned up.' She thought that was really funny. Then when she could speak better English she told us that she hadn't made the trousers she showed me that first day – it turns out she'd only put the pocket in! She used to work in a garment factory in Lithuania and it was her job to do the pockets and hems.

She's really funny, Stacey, and now we have this joke in the office where we say, 'Everyone lies to get a job. Remember you with the pocket, Stacey!' She goes mad when the girls say that to wind her up, but she's just hysterical. She's been with me since 2005 and her English is a lot better now.

Then there's Leanne. If you watch the TV show you'll recognise Leanne, she's the young blonde girl who does all the weddings with us. I've known Leanne since she was four years old, because Leanne is Pauline's daughter. She originally trained as a hairdresser and used to come and colour my hair when I was too busy to get to the salon.

Leanne started working for me when she was about 24. She had stepped in to look after the shop once while her mum went on holiday. She would sit and watch me decorating the corsets and kept asking me questions about it. 'I'd love to do something like that, Thelma,' she said.

'Why don't you give it a go?' I asked. I knew that Leanne was good at art. She was very creative and had taught crafts to under-privileged kids at the local youth club.

'Oh no, I might make a mess of it and waste all the crystals – I know they're really expensive,' she said.

I talked her into giving it a go and gave her a sample corset to practise on. It's great when you get someone who is a natural creative, because you can train people until you are blue in the face but if they haven't got the natural skill it shows. Of course, Leanne was brilliant at it. The only thing she really lacked was confidence, but I would work on that.

Since she started working for me Leanne has taken Nico to another level. Not only that, she also inherited her mum Pauline's determination and loyalty. And I have to admit that she reminds me of me at her age, full of imaginative ideas and passion for the task in hand.

Leanne is now the head designer at Nico and is starting to oversee parts of the process that I thought I had to do, which is great because it means that I can concentrate on other parts of the business. I used to feel that every one of my dresses was like my baby and that no one could do them as well as me – I am a bit of a control freak! – but I know now that the future of Nico is in Leanne's hands.

Now when the young traveller girls come in with their dress ideas and talk to us about the dresses they've seen in films, it is Leanne who works with them on the initial drawings. These sketches are then filed away until nearer the wedding date. We'll then do a first fitting and make a template corset of the girl's upper body.

This allows Yanli to start making the corset and Stacey can get on with the skirt. When the basic corset has been made it goes to Leanne, who will refer to the drawings and decorate it to create what the bride-to-be wants. She can create anything – flowers, butterflies, Baby Phat cats, swans, you name it. These will then be sewn on to the dress when Stacey's finished the skirt.

At that point the dress will go on the stand, and then Stacey will make the veil, the gloves and any other accessories that have been ordered – we now also make crowns, which was another one of Leanne's great ideas, and we are becoming known for these as much as we are for our wedding dresses.

When a dress is almost done, we'll look at the decoration on it, and if we think it looks nice then we know that the next thing we have to do is to double it. We know that if we do twice as much decoration then it will be just about right for our traveller girl's vision of what her dream wedding dress should look like.

We had a really funny moment in the workshop a few months ago when Leanne made this highly decorated head-dress to go with one of our wedding dresses. It was lovely, but when the girl came in she just looked at it, then looked at Leanne, and said, 'Oh no, now that's a bit much.'

When she left, none of us could move for laughing. 'That's it, Leanne,' I said. 'You've gone way too far!'

'I know, I must have if the travellers are telling me it's too much!' she laughed.

Often a girl will come in and say, 'I'm not like all the other travellers; I don't want loads of diamonds and loads of stuff on my dress. I really don't want my dress to look too much, you know?'

'OK, yeah,' we'll say, because we've heard that loads of times before. Then, more often than not, when the dress is getting to the final stages the girl or her mum says, 'I just want to add a few things.' And then it will be, 'Can I get a few more there?' And before you know it, it will be just as over the top as any other dress we've made.

'I thought you weren't like everyone else,' I'll say to them, laughing.

'Oh, no, what I mean, love, is that that's enough now,' the mum will say.

We've actually just had our first bride who didn't want any diamanté. Sometimes they'll say that to keep the price down, but usually, right at the end, they'll say, 'Go on then, put a few on,' thinking you're not going to charge them extra. But this girl, Delilah, really didn't want any embellishment at all. She just wanted a completely plain dress in white silk.

'Well,' I said to her, 'if you're not having any diamonds then you really should have some sort of design details, or the dress will look too bland.'

Leanne drew out a sketch for her. It was tailored like an old Christian Dior or an Alexander McQueen dress – I love the dresses Alexander McQueen made. It was quite sculptural and Leanne used lots of panels of pleats for the detail, to create different textures in the fabric. Delilah liked the idea of it and said she'd leave it to us.

We looked at some of the old Christian Dior dresses and found a picture of a dress where the pleats looked like fans coming out of the dress in criss-cross sections at the waist. We have a specialist that we go to for pleated details, and me and Leanne thought that something like that would work really well for this. And it did, it worked out lovely. It was so unusual.

Leanne went to the wedding to fit Delilah's dress, and afterwards she told us that everyone was going on about it and saying how amazing it was. It was really classy and people ask us about it all the time.

I think everyone was quite shocked at Delilah's whole take on her wedding, because she didn't wear a big crown either; she just had really simple flowers in her hair. But she was so pretty she didn't need anything else. It's the first time ever in all the years I've been doing this that a girl has said she didn't want any diamanté or decoration and genuinely meant it. And Delilah did look gorgeous in her dress.

Some dresses take longer than others to create. It really depends on the style and the amount of decoration a girl wants. If it involves making a new pattern, then obviously that takes longer, so we need to be really on top of the timings. But each of our dresses takes on average around 300 hours to complete.

The customer will first go into the shop and talk to Pauline about what they want and when. Most know they have to order at least six months in advance of the wedding date and book a start date in the diary first before sending their deposit. Only when that date has been booked, and the deposit paid, will we start talking to them about the order.

If the girls live in Ireland we don't ask them to come over for the first fitting. All we need are their measurements, and we don't usually ask them to come over until the last fitting. Because some of them have never been away from home, coming to the workshop to pick up their wedding dress is a really big deal for them. We tell them to come in a big van or car so they can fit everything in.

The Northern Irish traveller girls usually get engaged when they're 14 and book their start date far ahead, so we've got over a year before they get married. The Rathkeale girls get married in December, so they want us to start working on their dresses in March or April.

It's the ones who want it done in a few weeks that can cause us real headaches. These are the ones who have to get married quickly because the families are applying pressure, usually because the couple really like each other, and they want to prevent anything going on.

When we make a bride's wedding dress, we often find ourselves making one for her mother too. Now, because these girls get married so young, the mums are usually still really young themselves. So they'll come in and ask for outfits similar to what the younger girls want to wear, like a short skirt with a trail behind it and a corset. One mum, whose daughter was getting married at 16, wanted me to make up Cheryl Cole's wedding dress as her mother-of-the-bride outfit for the wedding. But then the mum was only 32 – and she looked amazing.

We also sometimes get asked to make engagement dresses, which are a bit like *Strictly Come Dancing* ballroom dresses – they are always really bright and are always *covered* in crystals.

We still make Communion dresses and the occasional christening dress as well, but they're not as big a part of the business as they used to be. But I do have a tradition in the shop where, if one of our brides has a baby girl, I'll make them the first christening robe for free. I don't do boys' ones, though, so they have to go somewhere else for that.

The only problem with that are the women who are always phoning me up trying to con the life out of me. They'll say, 'Ah, the baby turned out to be a boy, but her cousin had a girl, so can she get it?' They try to work it out, any which way they can, so that somebody will get that free christening dress. Still, I like the fact that they have the cheek to think anything's worth a try.

It's like when we loan out the underskirts for the dresses. We take a £500 deposit and give it back to them as soon as they bring the underskirts back. But we end up having the same argument every time.

'Don't forget your deposit for the underskirts,' we'll tell the girls before they come in to pick up the wedding dress. 'OK,' they say. But when it comes to it, it's always, 'Sorry, love, I haven't got enough money for the underskirts. But I swear on my kid's life I won't forget to bring them back.' Or they'll offer me something like a driving licence or a family allowance book. 'You can cash that, love,' they'll say.

One woman, whose wedding was all paid for and done, just needed to settle up for the underskirts when she came to collect the dress. She didn't have any money on her but offered us her credit card. It was nine o'clock at night and the only card machine we have was at the shop, which Pauline held the keys for.

'You can't pay with your card as we haven't got a card machine here and I haven't got keys for the shop,' I told her.

'Why don't you go round the corner and get the money out of a cash machine?' Leanne said.

But the customer came up with some excuse about why she couldn't get the cash out until the following day. 'I'll leave the card with you,' she said.

'No, no,' I said. 'I'm not going to be responsible for your card.'

'I trust you, love,' she said. 'I'll leave you my card with the pin number, and then tomorrow morning you can go and get the cash.'

By this time it was late and we were all really tired and desperate to get home. 'All right then,' I said, but even as she was walking out I was kicking myself. 'Why have I just done that?' I thought. I was convinced I'd never see those under-skirts ever again.

So the next morning I put the card in the machine and tried to take the £500 deposit, but it was declined. So then I thought, 'Let's try £250 and see if that works.' Declined again. Then I tried £100, and that went through, and another £100, which also went through. I think we got £220 in the end. 'Well, at least that's something,' I thought.

But then a couple of days later the woman's daughter did bring the underskirts back. I told her that we only got half of the money off the card, so that's what I'd pay back. But the girl wouldn't take it, 'My mum said to keep that as a deposit for a Communion dress for her granddaughter,' she told us.

A couple of hours later Pauline came into the workshop. 'We've just had a phone call,' she said. That woman had only gone and reported us to the police for stealing her credit card. I couldn't believe it. 'Shit,' I was thinking, 'I really don't need this. I've already been done for fraud.'

She told them we stole her card. Honest to God.

In the end she admitted to them that that wasn't what happened, and I think they cautioned her for wasting police time, but I wasn't best pleased.

Then, a few weeks later, the same woman left a message on the answerphone: 'Hi, Thelma, will you get back in touch with me? I want to talk to you about this Communion dress.'

11

The Tale of the Size 26 Bridesmaid

There's no doubt about it, gypsy women are tough. Life on the move with a family can't be easy, and these women have to deal with that. And, like in most societies, it's the women that ultimately keep the communities together by just making sure that all the day-to-day stuff is working. I've often wondered if it's the fact that traveller women's lives mainly revolve around the domestic side of things that gives their families some sense of stability.

Lots of people say to me that they can't believe how some traveller girls are pulled out of school to run the family home and how wrong they think it is that these young girls are made to do all the cooking and cleaning when their big sisters get married and leave. But that's the life a gypsy girl expects and I'd say that, from my conversations with them, it's what most of the girls want. And they definitely all want to get married – that is a big, big thing in their lives.

My Facebook page is filled with posts from girls saying, 'Oh, my sister got asked for last night.' They all get excited when someone in their family gets asked for, because they know that her wedding day is just around the corner.

Since I started working with gypsies, and Irish travellers in particular, the things I hear about their lives have often reminded me of that John Wayne film from the 1950s, *The Quiet Man*. It's set in Ireland and it's all about how this teenage girl, played by Maureen O'Hara, has to do everything that her brother tells her because they don't have a dad and so the brother is the head of the family. Her job is to do all the work in the house, all the cleaning and cooking, and she spends the whole film fighting for her independence.

For traveller women, keeping their home looking tiptop is a very important part of their lives. A gypsy woman's caravan is her pride and joy, and that's why the girls are taught to clean and bleach from a very young age. I've been in some amazing caravans now, and often it's like walking into a doll's house because everything is in miniature, even the cooker and the table. And most of them have thousands of ornaments. Every time I walk into one like that, I imagine having to dust all these trinkets every day. It must take bloody hours! And I'm terrible for knocking things over, so I'm always nervous when I go into the caravans.

I suppose a lot of people think that gypsy girls are treated as second-class citizens. But as she gets older and has more kids a gypsy woman's status grows. She becomes a matriarch figure, and the more kids she has, the more respect she gains. It's all about being a wife, a mother and a homemaker. And that's why a traveller girl's wedding day is so, so important: because when she's married she can start a family of her own.

That's also why her aim is to get asked for as soon as possible. A traveller girl will dress up to get noticed when she goes to family weddings, because that's where she has the best chance of getting to know a fella and meeting her future husband. So the girls come to Nico for wedding party outfits as well as wedding dresses. For these they'll ask us to design the most attention-grabbing outfit, in the brightest colour, with the most sparkle. Because they are all so young and pretty, every single one of them has to work hard to stand out.

The Northern Irish girls mostly go for short skirts, with a corset on top and maybe a trail at the back, all covered in crystals. Then they'll put lots of accessories in their hair, like feathers and clasps. They like to look like exotic birds.

People always ask me, 'Why do these girls go for such mega-sexy clothes when they are not even allowed to kiss a boy before they are married? It doesn't make sense.' Well, I can understand why some people might look at these girls and think, 'They're asking for it, wearing an outfit like that,' but it's all just show. Many people may consider the way these young girls dress as being outrageous and provocative. But the gypsies don't see revealing or sexy clothes as being bad. It's just dressing up to them; a form of showmanship.

Quite a few of the orders we make are for guests at weddings or girls looking for 'grabbing dresses'. Grabbing is what travellers call it when single young fellas at weddings try to get a kiss from the girl they fancy. It's not a tradition as such, it's a courting ritual, which I've been told only started happening around twenty years ago, and apparently not all traveller communities even do it. Grabbing outfits tend to be very sexy-looking, and the girls want them really tight, usually with cut-out shapes – cut away at the waist, maybe, or with a big slash down the middle. Or some ask us for belly tops and big belts.

The grabbing ritual can look quite rough, as a boy will sometimes drag a girl about in a way that she doesn't seem very happy about, maybe taking her out to the car park at a wedding and trying to kiss her. It can look quite barbaric. And when they screened the episode of *Big Fat Gypsy Weddings* that was all about grabbing, it caused a real storm. One of the producers had called me up a few days before it went out to warn me that the show was going to be a bit controversial, or 'near the knuckle', as he put it.

He was worried that there might be a backlash. And, of course, there was. There was loads written in the papers about it, and I got a few calls from other gypsies saying how outraged they were to see their community portrayed like that. They were keen to point out that grabbing is not something that all gypsies do.

All I would say, as someone who has seen this ritual up close many times, is that I don't think it's anything more than teenagers just playing around. From what I've seen, it's more of an attention-grabbing antic, or a game. I've sat outside hotels at weddings watching girls getting grabbed all round the car park, and it's literally just a kiss that the boys want, that's all.

Also, what you don't see on TV is that usually, when this is going on, all the families are milling about as well. The girls' brothers and cousins are there, so nothing's going to happen to them – nothing does happen to them. On telly you only see close-ups of the grabbing bit; you never see the other stuff that goes on around the situation, or the outcome.

I once saw a young bridesmaid get picked up and grabbed – she was probably only about 12, but she looked about 15 or 16 because of the way she was dressed – and one of the other girls immediately went in to get the girl's mum. The mum came out and went round the back of the hotel and found her with this lad. We were in an upstairs room, where we had fitted the dresses, and from the window I could see there was nothing going on, they were just mucking around. Anyway the mum handled it in a minute, without any fuss. 'Walk on, Mary Kate!

Walk on, Mary Kate!' she said, and her daughter giggled and followed her mum back into the wedding party.

That's not to say that I haven't seen a grab go wrong. We were sitting at a wedding once and a fella came right up in front of us and grabbed this girl off the dance floor. He just swooped in and picked her up. She obviously didn't want to go with him and struggled to get out of his grip. She got hold of someone next to her and tried to pull away, but he just kept pulling her. The table got knocked over and she fell and banged her head. But that was a one-off.

At one wedding I got talking to the groom and he told me that he'd been grabbing his wife for about twelve months. Every time they were at a wedding she knew he was going to grab her and give her a kiss, and she looked forward to it, because she liked him as much as he liked her.

Another time there was a girl of about 13 who was being filmed by one of the TV directors. Suddenly she started crying and asking him to help her get away from this lad who was grabbing her, saying that she didn't want to go. He helped her get him away. 'I couldn't sit back and watch that,' he told me.

'I know where you're coming from,' I said, 'but you've got to remember that a lot of it is all about the drama and getting attention. It's their way.' The thing is, these girls are so young, and often they have a tendency to be dramatic and over-emotional, like many teenage girls. I have seen them crying so much that you're thinking, 'Oh my God, I need to stop this.' Then two seconds later they'll turn around and chat away like normal. It's hard to understand the culture when you are just looking in on it from the outside, but you'd soon know if someone was really in trouble.

Anyone who watched the TV series might remember seeing a blonde girl called Cheyanne. It shows her shopping for a grabbing outfit and talking about what grabbing is, and about the place on the promenade where all the teenage lads go for grabbing. Then you see her getting grabbed off by this young lad, John, and her friend just walking away. It looked very dramatic, but if she was actually hurt there is no way her friend would have left her there. The next thing you see is Cheyanne crying and saying how no one likes grabbing and all that. Not long after, Cheyanne and John got engaged. And from what I hear they are very much in love.

So that's the whole reason these girls pay so much attention to their grabbing outfits. But while their mums and dads don't bat an eyelid when they turn up wearing their outrageous dresses, the girls wouldn't dare ask me to make them one in front of them. If a girl asks me to do a sexy dress, I'll say, 'Like a grabbing outfit?' but if her mum's there, she'll protest, 'No, no, not like that,' and give me a look to hush me up!

If the girl was to admit that the outfit she has ordered was for grabbing, it means that they've kissed one of these boys, and they would never talk about that with their mum. These girls would never discuss sex with their mum. They don't even talk freely about that with their husbands. As for the traveller boys, none of them know about periods or anything like that.

You see, the girls have a lot of respect for their mums, and the mums just love their kids, which is why they want their girls to have whatever it is they want. Sometimes, though, a girl will be a bit too cheeky or spoilt and talk back to her mum. Or she'll start getting really feisty and say, 'It's *my* wedding and this is what *I* want. I'll say what I'm having.' Then there are the pushy mothers whose daughters are very quiet, so the wedding becomes all about what the mother wants. But then I'm sure that most people would recognise those personality traits when it comes to wedding planning.

The difference with the weddings I deal with is that, no matter what, there's always a drama. I remember pulling up to the workshop one day and, as I was locking the car door, all I could hear were these God-awful screams coming from inside. 'What the hell is going on?' I thought as I put my key in the lock. I walked in to see a woman holding a young girl by her hair and banging her head against the shelves.

Pauline was screaming, 'Get off her, get off her!' and this woman was effing and blinding at the girl and telling her that she was going to knock her teeth out. This was the mother of the bride – with her daughter.

'Come on, come on,' I said and pulled the mum away. I led her into the office to try and get her to calm down, and she was swearing and cursing about this girl and going on and on. I left her for a minute so that I could go back and see how the girl was. As I walked into the other room the kid just started wailing and wailing. She was only 16 and she was crying her eyes out.

'Listen, babe,' I said. 'Everyone's nervous and stressed, but just try to calm down, it'll all be OK.'

'I know, I know,' she said, sniffling. Then, quick as you like, she started behaving like nothing had happened, as though she were auditioning for a play. 'Can I have a look at the skirt?' she asked, turning to the dress. 'Have you put the same decoration on the after skirt?'

'Can I have a look at the skirt?' I thought, shocked at her nonchalance. 'You've just been battered!' Here was me, thinking, 'That poor girl's going to be traumatised for years to come by what her mother's just done to her.' But no, like most of my dealings with traveller girls, it seemed it was all about the performance.

Another time we had a situation involving a mum and dad. We'd finished all the dresses for a wedding and the bride and her dad had come to pick them up. When it came to settling up, he asked how much he owed us. When Pauline told him, he hit the roof and started calling his wife every name under the sun. 'That effing bitch – she never told me it was going to be that much!'

Then he got on the phone to his wife and, in front of us and his kids – the bride and her brother – started screaming at her, using swear words that I've never heard before in my life. I stood there listening to him screaming down the phone, then I tried to butt in and get him to calm down. 'Now look, maybe she didn't realise that's what it would be,' I said, but it was hard to get his attention.

All this time his kids are just talking away to each other like nothing's going on, even though their dad is giving their mother merry hell. You end up standing there looking at all this play-acting, thinking, 'My God, what a drama!' So then the dad gets off the phone and just looks at me and says, 'OK, love, thanks for that.'

This is so typical of the travellers' ways: they make huge dramas out of nothing and then think nothing of huge dramas.

Of course, when we first started experiencing all these scenes in the workshop, we were all gobsmacked. But it seems normal to us now. We know that everything the travellers do looks and sounds worse than it is and, it might sound hard to believe, but I'd say that gypsies live in happy families generally. They may not seem very functional by some standards, but to me the actual set-up of gypsy homes seems to be a lot more stable than many of those in settled communities. The mum and dad and the kids stick together. If you do find a single-parent family, it's usually only because either the dad or the mum has died. So their kids have got the best of their mum and dad. I think that kind of family is becoming rarer in settled societies.

Aside from all the drama, we do end up having very good relations with the girls and their families. Most of the brides are really, really lovely girls and sweet-natured with it. They become quite close to us too, and I suppose because their mums don't go out to work or have a particular role, the girls confide in us about things that they can't talk to the other women in their communities about. To some of them we become like surrogate mums.

Over the years we've had a couple of pregnant traveller girls come to us. None of them had told anyone else about what was happening, because if it's found out that they are pregnant before they get married that would be really looked down upon. Once a girl is married, it's fine. Even if she had the baby three weeks after the wedding, no questions would be asked. But if anyone finds out before, it reflects badly on a girl's mum, and these girls hate to let their mums down. But they tell us. They have to, because if they're expecting, the fact is that they are going to get bigger, so the tight corset and the skirt might not fit.

I remember this one girl called Annie. We knew her already, as she was supposed to have been married the year before but the wedding was put on hold. We still had the dress, but it wasn't finished, and we hadn't heard anything from her or the family in months.

Months later she finally called to ask if she could come and get the dress, even though she was worried that it might not fit her. I said that we could only alter it so much, considering the stage it was at, and we couldn't remake it as we were just too busy with other weddings. She said she'd put on weight, so I told her I was happy to give her deposit back. She pleaded with me to do it for her, but I told her that we couldn't fit it in.

That weekend I had popped into the office to pick something up. There was a knock on the door. When I opened it, Annie was just standing there sobbing her heart out, and the next moment she was hanging off my neck. 'God, what's the matter?' I asked.

She was shaking. 'Please do my dress, Thelma, please do it.'

'I can't, Annie love,' I said. 'We've got back-to-back weddings over the next couple of weeks and we're not going to have time. Put your date back and we can do it after all the other ones.'

'I want to tell you something,' she said. 'Please don't tell anyone. Promise you won't tell anyone. I'm pregnant.'

'All right, I'll do it,' I said.

We'd already made the corset – but she'd had a 22-inch waist when she first came to us. So I told her that there was no way in this world that it was going to fit her now.

'I don't care,' she said.

'No, what's important, Annie, is that you're having a baby,' I said to her. 'Forget the tight corset. I'll make you a new one.' I had to make alterations to the skirt too. Really, I should have charged her for all the extra work I had to put in, but her mum would have wanted to know why the price had gone up. I was sworn to secrecy and out of pocket with it.

Another bride came in and said: 'One of my bridesmaids is pregnant, so she's not doing it now. But, you know, I've got this other one who's going to do it instead.'

'Well, as long as she is the same size, that's fine,' I said.

'Yeah,' she said, 'she is.'

So, in she comes with this other girl. Only she's a size 26! 'Well,' I said, 'if she's going to be your bridesmaid, her dress is going to cost you double!'

'Why's that? Oh, don't be like that!' she said.

'It's going to be double because it's going to be double the decoration, double the fabric, double everything, so either drop her or think again,' I said.

'But I can't,' she said. 'It's my boyfriend's sister.'

I gave her a rough idea of the price it would be, but she wasn't having any of it. 'Oh, come on, come on, just do us a deal,' the girl kept saying when I told her what it would cost.

'I can't do a deal because it's a different pattern altogether,' I said. 'How can I make this girl a dress for the same price as your other bridesmaids? It's just not going to happen. And, you know, she's going to look stupid with a see-through corset on as well; it won't look good on her shape. She'll look ridiculous. Do you want people to laugh at her? To laugh at your wedding?'

'Oh, but it's a corset,' she said. 'It'll pull her in.'

'Yeah, but it's got to push out somewhere else – she's just going to come out over the top,' I explained.

It might sound like I'm being harsh, but you've got to tell it to people straight sometimes. Luckily the gypsies prefer that, and so do I.

But then it's the same for any dressmaker: women putting on or losing weight is a big deal when you are making dresses to order. And if people are particularly overweight it can really affect the cost, as it will involve more fabric and decoration, and that means higher labour costs too.

We've learned this the hard way, because when we work on a wedding the order usually adds up to more than ten dresses, often many more, as there are the bridesmaids and guests to do too. So now there are certain families that we won't take an order from because we know that they are all too overweight.

Then there are the times when we're told that a bridesmaid is seven or eight years old, and she turns out to be the size of a 15-year-old – a woman's size. I had one bridesmaid who had a 42-inch chest and a 40-inch waist, so now I try to avoid doing really big bridesmaids. I really don't mean to sound cruel, but it's also my job to manage the girls' ideas and expectations.

I do try to be as nice as I can about it if someone comes in asking us to make a dress for a big bridesmaid, as we all know what it feels like to worry about weight. I'll tell the bride or the bride's mother a price for all their bridesmaids' dresses and then let them know that whoever is the bigger size will need a bigger size dress, which means double the decoration, double the time and double the price.

'But why, love? Why?' they'll always say.

'Well, I can't tell you any straighter than that,' I always tell them, and I'll gently put it to them that they might suggest the girl goes on a diet – loads of people diet for weddings, so I think that's quite reasonable.

I remember this girl, Elizabeth, who came in and was complaining to me about a price that Pauline had given her. Now she was dead pretty, but she was on the large side. 'If Pauline's given you the price, then that's the price it is,' I said, without even looking at the piece of paper given to her by Pauline that she had in her hand.

'But it's ridiculous, really ridiculous,' she kept on.

So I looked at the price and it certainly was much higher than normal. 'Well, the reason she's charging you that, Elizabeth, is because of the size of your dress,' I said. 'We could make three dresses by the time we've made yours.'

'You cheeky bitch,' she said. 'Right, well, I'm going to go on a diet,' she huffed.

I have to say, I've heard that from quite a few girls. And usually when they come back they've put on weight rather than lost it. So I told her, 'Come back when you've dieted and we'll talk about the price. Actually, I tell you what, if you get down to a size 10 I'll give you the dress for nothing.'

'I will!' she said.

And she did.

Six months later she turned up with a perfect size 10 figure. We were made up for her and, as promised, we made her dress for her for free. 'You look really amazing,' we all told her. 'You deserve it,' I said.

She was delighted, as she told me that if I hadn't said that to her she wouldn't have done it. She really wanted that dress and my straight talking had given her the incentive to lose the weight she'd struggled with for years.

It goes the other way too. A lot of the traveller girls are really slightly built – because they are so young they don't have any fat on them at all, which means they often have no boobs and no bum.

We had one 16-year-old bride who was really worried that her after-party dress was going to fall down because she had no bum. So we went out and got this padded false bum – like a Wonderbra but with more padding in it.

And, yes, her bum did look big in it! She loved it.

For a few weeks after that wedding we had loads of calls from traveller women asking the same thing: 'Is this where you get the false bums?'

12

The Tale of the Bartering Brother

'How much does a dress cost?'

If I had a pound for every time someone asked me that, I'd be a very rich woman. It's the one thing that everyone wants to know and the thing I can never, ever tell. None of the big fashion designers like Chanel and Dior would ever reveal what a customer pays for a couture dress, and it's the same with us: all our dresses are made to order, so really it's impossible to put an exact price on them.

Maybe that's another reason why gypsies like working with us – we don't do fixed prices. When it comes to money, travellers always have to do a deal. They never work to set costs, and I had to learn this quickly when working with them.

Gypsies love to barter. Mary, who gave me my first wedding dress order all those years ago at Paddy's, taught me a lot about that.

I used to get really stressed about haggling when I first started working with travellers. I remember being embarrassed for them too. I mean, when you see something in a shop and it says '£10' on it, that's what you pay – you don't go to the till and start arguing about the price and trying to get them to knock something off, do you? So I was quite scared whenever anyone said, 'Will you do me a deal?'

Even when you do offer to do something for less, the travellers want you to go lower still. I can't tell you the number of times I've been told, 'Oh, but that's all I've got. I've got three more daughters to get married, you know.' When I hear these words I know I'm going to be standing there haggling for at least a couple of hours. Every time. Without fail.

Years ago, when we'd just started at Nico, this woman came in to pay for some dresses. Everything was done and we'd agreed the price, but when it came to paying she just kept saying, 'But I've given you every penny I've got, love. We've given you a load of money there. We've given you everything we've got. Please, love – I'll pay you after the wedding.'

And I'm thinking, 'Yeah …'

Eventually, she said, 'Look, I'll leave you my Rolex.'

Well, I knew she'd come back for that, so I said that that was OK and we took the Rolex. We agreed that she'd come back two weeks later with the underskirts we'd lent her and the money for the extra stuff, and I would give her watch back.

When she didn't come back, I thought, 'I don't care – I've got a Rolex there that's worth more than what she owes me.' So I was looking at it and saying to Pauline, 'It's definitely real, you can see the movement on it.' We couldn't wait to find out how much it was worth, so Pauline took the watch down to the local jewellers. Of course, it wasn't worth a carrot! It was a fake. Pauline couldn't stop laughing as I'd been so convinced that we were on to a winner. Needless to say, it doesn't take us a minute to spot the con merchants now.

Which is just as well because, apart from the actual designing and making of the dresses, the money side of things is probably the biggest part of what we do and it takes up a lot of our time.

The thing is, the gypsies want to know the price of everything the minute they walk through the door. As soon as we've agreed on the dress design, they want the cost, right there and then. But they always, always add more details on throughout the dressmaking process. And they seem not to understand that we don't just stick these things on with superglue – making them and crafting them on to the dress takes time, which is an extra cost. They just can't get their heads around that. In their eyes, a dress is a dress, no matter how opulent, carefully made or intricate it is. And no matter how long it takes to make.

I've learned to deal with that, though, and now I have a bit of a system on the go. I will cost a dress out for them and then quote them a higher price that allows for the bargaining bit. In my head I know the very lowest price that I'm going to go to, and they basically know what they're prepared to pay – and we usually meet somewhere in the middle. And that's it. Generally, it works, and everyone walks away happy.

But that's the easy part. It can take an awfully long time to get to that point. In the early days we began to notice a pattern when it came to the costing side of things. The girls would come in with their families and they'd all know exactly what they were looking for. But these girls are only 15 and 16, so when they get to the workshop and see everything going on around them, the dresses on stands, the diamanté, the gorgeous fabrics, they are like kids in a candy shop. They have no idea about money and what things cost, so they go on and on and on about wanting a whole lot of other things on their dresses.

Now I say to them, after the first half-hour's discussion, 'Listen, I'm not going to sit here drawing you twenty-five dresses out. Tell me your budget, then we can draw it.'

'Oh I don't know my budget, but I want this, this, and this …' They don't get that every new detail takes time and money to make. In the end you will have drawn out, to the very last detail, the dress they want, and given them a price. Then, without fail, the mum will look at it and say: 'Oh, I can't afford that, love.'

'I just told you that!' I'll say.

So we have to get the dress we sketched out at the first meeting and say, 'Right, what do you want us to take off?'

The mother will say, 'Take the flowers off.'

Then the daughter will pipe up: 'But will you make me a bracelet?'

'So, which of you am I listening to here?' I ask, butting in, trying to get them to stop for a minute. But they just carry on: 'But will you make me a crown?' They can never agree, and the mum's knocking as much off as she can while the daughter's just adding more stuff on every time she does.

We used to spend three or four hours with these girls while they created their fantasy dresses. Honestly, we literally had to listen to 'And I want this, and I want that ...' for hours.

Now I say straight away, 'What's your budget? Tell me your budget.' It's probably just as hard to get that out of them, though, and sometimes it just doesn't work at all. My other tactic is to say, 'Do you know what, you two go and have a coffee and have a talk about it. Go away and discuss what you want and then come back in an hour.' That tactic often gets a more up-front result.

Even so, we always have to try to pull the girls back to reality at some point. One girl came in and said: 'I want the whole skirt covered in Swarovski crystals.'

'OK now, shall we be sensible here?' I said to her. 'How are you going to walk in a dress like that?' I took some bags of

219

crystals out of the cupboard. 'Here are ten bags,' I said, putting them into her hands. 'Now, hold these. You'll be looking at around 550 times more weight than that. How the hell are you going to be able to walk in that? You're not going to be able to move.'

'OK,' she said, 'but as long as it's the best. I want it to be the best dress you've ever made.'

But then that's really all my traveller brides care about, having the biggest and the best dress that anyone's ever seen.

Yet, even after we've delivered that, things don't always go smoothly, as the travellers still want to haggle about the price – especially when the finished dress is made and ready to collect. There have been a couple of times that I've had to hold a dress to ransom because a girl's dad has refused to pay the agreed price, even though he's told me, 'Give her anything she wants.'

We made one of the most extravagant dresses we'd ever done for this girl Maria – the skirt, which was made from the best white silk-satin we could find, had thousands and thousands of Swarovski crystals on it and was really, really big. Another 40-feet circumference job, it looked like the girl was coming out of a giant, glittery Christmas bauble. As Leanne had made a huge crystal tiara and Swarovski-covered gloves to match, the overall effect was spectacular. In fact, you almost needed sunglasses to look at it. And, of course, with all that embellishment it weighed a ton.

A couple of days before the wedding, once the dress was complete, in all its spectacular glory, her dad, John, called up and asked how much he owed. When I told him, he said, 'No way, no. You can do it for less than that.'

I'd gone as far down as I was prepared to go. 'No,' I told him, 'you're not on, John. We've done the deal.' I was arguing with him for what felt like the whole day. 'Look,' I said, 'I've done the dress and the after-outfit and your other daughter's got an outfit too.' But he still wanted to knock me down further. He wanted hundreds more pounds off. Now, I'm used to bartering, but not to that extent. I had to really dig my heels in this time, in a way that I'd never had to before.

'Do you know what? Forget it,' he said. 'The wedding's off!'

'That's entirely up to you, John,' I told him. 'It doesn't bother me.'

'Well, I'll give you until two o'clock to make your mind up,' he told me. 'Phone me by two o'clock if you want the money for the dress.' It was two days before the wedding.

I laughed. 'I'll tell you what, you'll be waiting a long time to hear from me. You won't be getting *any* phone call', I said, 'because that's what we agreed and I'm not going to change my mind.'

And I didn't phone him. But I remember thinking, 'Oh God, I've made all this stuff,' and we'd all been working on it for about six or seven weeks by then. My stomach started turning. That dress cost us a fortune to make. You know, it takes long enough to make any of our dresses, but this was just unbelievable and me and Pauline and the girls had been working flat out – sometimes till four in the morning. We just had to finish it. It had to be done. It just had to be ready for that girl's wedding day.

When two o'clock came John phoned to make me another offer. He thought I'd take it because he knew I'd made everything by then.

But I wasn't having it this time. 'No, you're not getting the dress until you give me the amount that we agreed,' I said. 'So go ahead and call it all off.' By that point I'd been thinking about the fact that his daughter Maria was the apple of her daddy's eye and quite spoilt. I knew she wouldn't let him call it off. So I stuck to my guns.

At five o'clock he phoned me back. 'I'm sending a driver down with the money now if you accept my last offer,' he said. He'd asked me to lower the price again, but I said no, and told him that as long as the lad came to the workshop with the full money I'd give him the dress, but he wouldn't get anything otherwise. He finally relented and later that day a driver turned up with the full money. So we loaded the dress into the van and headed for the venue.

When we got to the wedding Maria was just so happy with it, and she looked beautiful in that dress. Now, the thing is, this was the second dress we'd done for her, because she'd been married before and we'd had no trouble with her dad when it came to paying the last time. In fact, I'd always got on well with John. So I went over to talk to him at the wedding and I was just about to say, 'I can't believe the way you did that,' when Davey came up and told me that it was him who had called me, not his dad. All that stress because the young lad was just inexperienced at haggling – or a better business-man, I suppose, depending on how you look at it.

Generally, as I've said, the dads don't get so involved, though it's not unusual, when we do a girl's dress, for them to come to the first meeting, so that we can talk about the money side of things after we find out what it is the girl wants. At the start we'll sit with her and work out the design that she is hoping to get. We'll ask the dad to come back later, so that when it's all agreed we can take him into the office and tell him the price. At that point the dad will always say, 'No, no, it's too much.' So we'll say, 'OK, right, so what we can do is take this bit of detail off and that will bring the price down.'

So then we bring the girl back in again. 'Your dad doesn't want to pay that much, so to knock the price down we can't do this and we can't do that,' I'll tell her.

Of course she doesn't want that to happen because she wants the biggest and the best. It's all about the adding on, so taking anything away is just not on her agenda. And this is the rigmarole we go through every time:

'No, no, no, I want that on,' she'll cry.

'Oh, go on, love, how much for the way it is?' he'll ask.

'I've just given you the price for the way it is,' I say.

'No, no, love. Just tell me – what's the price?'

I'll then go through it all again: 'If you want it cheaper you're going to have to knock something off the design.'

'I don't want nothing off!' the girl will shout. And it goes on and on like that while they try to get the price down. You know, sometimes I feel like I'm becoming more experienced at haggling than I am at making dresses.

There was this one girl who came in with her brother – her dad was dead. The mum had been around at the start but now the brother was coming in to pick up and pay for the dress.

'You know, this is a lot of money for just one day,' he said to me.

'Well, that's not my problem,' I told him, thinking to myself, 'Every bloody wedding dress is meant for just one day. Do you think people should get married more than once just to get their money's worth?'

'Look, I've already done the deal with your mum, right, so this is it,' I said. But, as usual, he went on and on for ages trying to knock the price down.

Eventually I had to put a stop to it, so I looked straight at him. 'Listen, tell you what we'll do,' I said. 'We'll toss for it.' He owed us thousands – we'd done all the outfits for the flower girls, bridesmaids and pageboys too – and I was offering to toss for it! That's what happens sometimes, you start doing crazy things, thinking of desperate measures, just to bring a deal to a close; just to get some peace. Otherwise you could be standing there bartering until your dying day.

'OK,' he said, 'yeah.'

'So we'll toss, and if you lose you pay me double, right. And if I lose, you take everything away for nothing. OK?' I suggested.

'Go on then. We'll do it,' he said.

I don't know who looked more nervous, me or him, but we were both desperate not to show it. So we got a coin and found someone in the shop to toss it. Of course, the traveller fella wants to have a look at the coin first: 'Let's see the coin. Let's see it,' he goes, turning it over and over in his hand and looking at it. I was just waiting for him to bite into it.

Finally he says, 'No, no, I'm not doing it.'

'But you just said that you wanted to toss for it,' I said. 'You pay me double, right – but before we do, put your double money on the table – or if you win you just take the dress and everything away and keep the money. It's that simple.'

He stood there for what felt like about an hour, just thinking about it. Then he said, 'No, no, I'll just pay the money. I'll give you the money.'

'All right, it's up to you,' I said. So he paid us everything he owed and then, just before he was about to leave, I turned to him and said, 'Shall we toss just to see who would have won?'

'Yeah, go on then,' he said. So we tossed it – and he would have won. He was like, 'Aarghh.' But we both had a laugh.

The funny thing is, because travellers like to barter so much, I've had situations before where someone has nearly ended up paying more than we first agreed. 'I think I just said a lower price and you're coming back with a higher one,' I'll say. 'What's going on?'

And they'll go, 'Oh yeah. I didn't mean that.'

They just love the banter. Especially the men. When they come in with the daughters and wives to pay, the first thing they say to me is, 'Oh, you must be raking it in.' They all want to talk about business and how much money I'm making. It's all to do with the money. 'Oh, you must be a millionaire by now, you must be,' they say, looking at me, as if I'm going to say, 'Yeah, yeah, I am. I'm a millionaire, that's right.'

I think it's just hard for anyone – and not just travellers – to understand the amount of work and time that goes into what we do. People think you just run up a bit of fabric on a sewing machine. If only it was as easy as that; then I really would be a millionaire.

Actually, we've made dresses for quite a few millionaire traveller families in the past, but the wealthiest of all are the Rathkeale families. Towards the end of every year hundreds of gypsies travel to this little town near Limerick in southern

Ireland where they have homes. We only began to realise that Rathkeale travellers were different from our regular traveller families when we started getting loads of orders for December weddings. Last year we did thirteen Rathkeale weddings in one week.

We first noticed it about four years ago when this particular crowd of girls used to come in and talk about weddings in December. They'd come in and ask, 'Have any of our girls been in?' I used to look at them and think, 'Your girls? I don't know!' I had no idea what they were talking about. But we didn't realise then they were from another part of the community; we just thought they were Irish, until one day it just clicked. It was the way they talked again. Their language was kind of old-fashioned and they'd say 'mama' instead of mammy and 'dada' instead of daddy. It's hard to explain, but when they spoke it sounded as though they were people who lived 100 years ago.

We also began to notice that there was a pattern with the dates, and although we didn't know Rathkeale existed we knew that there were all these weddings around that time. In fact, the Rathkeale travellers have all their celebrations – engagements, weddings, First Communions in December – before they go off travelling again in January.

Then we realised that these girls actually dressed differently from other travellers too: they cover up more – they'll wear their skirts over their knees, that sort of thing. They also have to have a chaperone at all times; they are not allowed to be on their own at all in case they go off with boys.

Rathkeale family rules are very, very strict. And while the girls still marry young, the men tend to be older. The men are like 30 and the girls are 16. And they all marry within other Rathkeale families, not even other travellers. So they all hang about together.

It's a really wealthy little town and the houses are all massive. There's a tradition of travellers owning houses in Rathkeale, and the local cemetery is filled with related gypsy family names – and some very grand-looking headstones.

And yet the families are there less than three months of the year – from the end of November to January; they travel the rest of the time, quite often across the world. When they leave, most of the houses are boarded up, and Rathkeale becomes a ghost town.

The other thing that struck us as strange about the Rathkeale travellers was when they started talking about dowries. When we heard talk of that, we knew they were different from the other Irish travellers. 'Come on, give me a good deal, I've got a big dowry to pay,' a father might tell us.

Pauline and me would be looking at each other, thinking, 'A dowry? What do you mean, a dowry? Do people still pay those?'

'Oh well, it's the youngest son that she's marrying, so we've got to pay a big dowry,' he'd say.

'Oh my God,' I thought. 'I can't believe what I'm hearing here. It's like the dark ages.'

Rathkeale families seem prosperous. There's a lot of wealth around and they are very respected by the other travellers. Some of the families run antiques or wine businesses, and lots travel the world working when they are not in Ireland.

Some of our regular customers got really excited when we told them that we were going over to do our first wedding there, so we knew that it would be something different. 'Make sure you look in the graveyard,' they said. Be sure you do this, go and see that. 'Go and have a look at the Sheridans' house, it's the big one on the hill.' The Rathkeale families are gypsy A-listers – the Brads and Angelinas of the traveller world.

I'll never forget the first wedding we did there. It was a clear, sunny December day and the drive up to the town was beautiful. Then we got to a point where we couldn't drive past because the road was blocked with every type of luxury car you can think of – Porsches, BMWs, the lot. They were all coming down this country lane with their horns going. All these teenage traveller kids were driving the cars, stopping and chatting to the young girls who were walking up the road – unlike the Romany girls with their dark hair and big blue eyes, the Rathkeale girls have a pale look, with red hair and freckly skin, and most of them are very skinny. So all these kids in their flash cars were stopping and waving to each other. There was no way we were going to get through without a bit of a wait. But then there was so much for us to take in – we were mesmerised.

I remember seeing two really old men wearing flat caps sitting on a bench in that little country town, quietly taking this scene in. They must have been thinking, 'What the hell is going on?' All the young kids were beep-beep-beeping and shouting to each other and revving up their engines. It was a real sight to see, shocking in a way. We'd never seen anything like it.

Now there are around nine to fifteen weddings there every year. The last time we went, this woman came running out of her house to show us a picture of one of her girls we'd made a dress for when she was a kid. It was a really flouncy, little pink thing – olde-worlde-looking and sweet. You see, the Rathkeale gypsies still like traditional-looking outfits for their little ones. But when it comes to the wedding dresses they ask for some of the craziest designs, probably because they have biggest budgets. The sisters who wanted the pineapple and palm tree dresses were Rathkeale customers.

They had been living in Spain for a while and loved the idea of reliving their time in the sun with a tropical-style party before the wedding. So we all sat down and came up with the ideas for the dresses together – though the bride-to-be's 16-year-old sister was the one with the boldest notion of what she wanted.

And between the three of us we actually worked that one out surprisingly quickly – though Leanne was left with all the technicalities of making it work in practice. For the palm tree dress for the bride we decided that the basic dress would be blue satin, to represent the sky, and the trunk of the tree would be in Piña Colada orange silk with Swarovski trimming, sweeping up the body from the hem to the right shoulder. The green leaves of the palm tree then spread out over the shoulder, like a corsage. The skirt was all frills and flounces, and looked like a Spanish flamenco dancer's dress.

For the pineapple bridesmaid we made the bodice with quilted yellow silk, fringed in crystals, so it actually looked like a pineapple. The fluorescent green leaves burst out of the bodice and the skirt was a giant luminous green fishtail that was removable, so that the young girl, Chantelle, could wear the pineapple midsection at the evening party as a mini-dress.

Leanne suggested adding some tropical flowers for the girls' hair, but they refused, saying that no one would understand what they were because you don't see flowers on palm trees and pineapples. The bride asked for a mini palm tree on her head instead.

Then there was the girls' mum, the mother of the bride; she wanted to be a coconut. Actually, that's a joke, but I seriously wouldn't have been surprised if she'd asked for that. She wanted a mix of the two girls' dresses and plumped for a sky-blue satin sheath-dress with a tulle fishtail in luminous green and yellow. She looked amazing in it. In fact, all three of them looked amazing, and I'll never forget the moment when the trio arrived at the party and everyone laid eyes on their outfits for the first time. No one turned a hair. It was like, 'Yeah, she's a palm tree,' and then all the guests just carried on talking as normal.

But then, Rathkeale really is like a world of its own. Just before we filmed there for the first time for *Big Fat Gypsy Weddings*, I got a text from one of the younger members of the crew that said: 'It's just like Disneyland here. It's unbelievable!' They had got there to find a jamboree going on – flashy cars everywhere, flags draped all around and parties happening in every house, every night. They said it was a million times more extravagant than they had expected; like nothing they had ever seen.

The strange thing is, while the usual Irish traveller wedding party might go on for days, the Rathkeale weddings last just a couple of hours. At a recent one we arrived at the reception hall at about twenty past four, after a four-hour drive from the church, and the entire wedding was over by six o'clock. Almost on the dot everyone started to leave, which felt strange. You see, with the Rathkeale travellers the big celebration – the joint stag and hen party – happens the night before the ceremony. And often there's another wedding happening the next day, so everyone's keen to head off to the next party.

They also usually want to pay by cheque or money transfer, unlike most of our traveller customers, who pay in cash.

At Nico we are often surprised by the gypsies who turn out to be extremely wealthy. There was one woman, who has been a customer of ours for years, who is really lovely and unassuming, and she asked us to come to her house in Ireland to do some fittings. When we got to the airport there was a chauffeur-driven Bentley waiting to pick us up. We were so surprised. Then we went to her house and it was just amazing, not what we expected at all. To look at her, you wouldn't have imagined her living the way she does. She was always lovely to work with, but she didn't show off and wasn't snobby or flashy about anything, even though she could have been. She just made us feel really welcome and pulled out all the stops.

Although sometimes it's the other way round; we've had traveller customers who look flamboyant and appear to be quite wealthy, but the reality has been the opposite. Last year, for example, we had an order for twenty bridesmaids' dresses. The family lived in Ireland and the bride's mum was keen to get them all properly fitted, so rather than have them all come over to Liverpool it made sense for one of us to go over to them, and we sent Leanne to do it.

Now, the dad of the family had made quite an impression on us. He was one of the first people in our experience to come into the workshop, ask how much the wedding dress would cost, pull the cash out there and then and put it on the table. No quibble about it, nothing. He wasn't even saying, 'OK, here's the deposit' – he just gave me the whole lot. And I suppose, because of this, we kind of assumed that they were loaded. And they'd also offered to pay for Leanne to fly over and do the fittings.

So, after the last time we went over, when we got picked up in the Bentley, Leanne thought that this family was going to live in a mansion. But when she got there she found that their home was just a little caravan. I was so surprised when she told me that, because when they had first travelled over to see us they arrived in one of those big motor homes. It must have cost a fortune, and yet they lived in this little tiny trailer. And when Leanne asked where the toilet was, she was told it was outside. She had to walk across a field in the dark to get there, because travellers don't tend to have toilets in their caravans as they think it's disgusting to have one so near their living space.

The thing I really like about the travellers, though, is that, whether it's a big house or a simple trailer we have been invited to, we have always been made to feel so welcome.

And that's worth everything to me.

13

The Tale of the Dancing Kids

I think the reason the gypsies we know are so warm and welcoming to us now is that we have been involved with many of the same families for years. I've watched their girls grow up, as one daughter's marriage has been followed by another. And I have worked with some girls from their Communion dresses right through to their wedding dresses. Maybe that's why some of the gypsy families see me as more than just a dressmaker – often I feel like I end up being like a family counsellor too.

Pinning a dress takes a while, and it's during this stage of the dressmaking process that you can become quite close to the girls and their mums. That's when you get a chance to chat – and, I have to say, gypsy women love to gossip.

I'll be measuring a girl up and her mum will be gabbing away: 'Do you know so and so?'

'Yeah,' I'll say. 'That's her with the four kids.'

'Yeah, that's right, her. Well, do you know who her fella has run off with?'

And then she'll carry on and tell me the scandal.

An hour later another woman from another family will come in and say, 'Now, love, don't say I told you, but her husband's run off ...' It will go on like this for weeks – all the women from different families telling you the same story but in different ways. It's like Chinese whispers.

Sometimes a man will come and pay for a dress for his daughter and tell me his wife will pick it up. Then his wife will come and tell me all about how her husband has run off with someone else and ask if she can get the money back for the dress as the wedding's in doubt because the dad's gone and done this, that and the next thing. So I end up right in the middle of it, trying to sort them all out.

It happens a lot when weddings are called off. One of the older women will come in and say, 'The wedding's off, it's all been called off, love. So you can tell his family when they come in for their outfits that I've been in and cancelled everything. Just tell them.' They won't even have told the husband-to-be. They want me to do it for them.

'I don't really want to get in the middle of this, you know,' I'll say. But then when the other mum – the groom's mum

– comes in to pick up her outfit, I have to tell her. 'Erm, did you know that she's cancelled everything?' I ask her.

'Oh, I don't understand this,' says the mum, looking only slightly put out. 'My son will make a fabulous husband and she's never going to get anyone as good as him.'

'Oh, I know,' I tell her, trying to make her feel better. But there's no fuss, no tears, no disbelief. She just accepts that it's off and that's it.

For as much as weddings are such a big deal to travellers, when one is called off, it's not. If that happened in a settled family, everyone would be shocked. But the travellers just take these kinds of things on the chin. All the events that would be such major dramas in other people's lives are like water off a duck's back to them.

But, of course, even if a wedding is called off, all the outfits still have to be paid for. As some of the kids are likely to get married to someone else pretty soon after, we often hang on to the dresses until the next one, so it usually works out for everyone and our customers are rarely left out of pocket in the end.

Not long after this particular incident I saw the woman who I'd had to tell about the wedding being off at another wedding. She recognised me and came over. 'I never wore that outfit, you know,' she told me, meaning the one that I had made for her to wear to her son's wedding.

'Oh, that's a shame,' I said.

And then she pulled me over to another table full of women. 'Tell her how good my sons are. You tell them what good husbands they'd make,' she said, pointing to me, then to the family. They just looked at her as though she was asking them how much they paid for a loaf of bread and let her go on.

Of course the women love their sons, but their daughters are their pride and joy, especially when it comes to their wedding day. The bride's mum, who is usually there for most of the dressmaking process, is determined that her baby girl should have the best of everything, even if her husband has restricted how much she is allowed to spend. It happens all the time. And these girls know how to twist their daddies round their little fingers.

We had one girl whose dad couldn't really control her, and her dress ideas just got bigger and bigger. It was pure fantasy, with more feathers and crystals than you can ever imagine you could fit on to one dress – even one as big as ours. We'd made a dress for her sister earlier in the year who was completely different. A very unassuming girl, she was quite happy to let the others fuss about, but she wasn't that bothered herself. She was just happy to be getting married to the boy she loved. But this sister, Theresa, was a bit spoilt.

One time we had to bring her into the office to tell her that, because she wanted a crown to match the dress, it was starting to cost more than her dad had said she could spend, so she'd have to get the OK from him before we went ahead. So she phoned him up.

'Oh, Daddy, Daddy,' she said, really pleading with him to let her have what she wanted. He obviously said no, or something to that effect. So this girl is crying so much she puts the phone down.

A couple of minutes later her phone rings. 'Now listen, Patrick,' she's saying. 'No, Patrick, I don't want that, Patrick.'

I was just looking at her, thinking that's a bit odd, maybe she's talking to her brother. So I asked her, 'Was that your brother on the phone this time?'

'No,' she said. 'It was my daddy. I call him Patrick when I'm annoyed with him.'

The girls always have this thing where they will turn to the dad and ask for more. It's always, 'Oh Daddy, will you let me have this? Will you?' The father might say no, but then he'll call me up and try to get me to give her what she wants even though he doesn't really want to pay any more money. Or he'll come into the workshop and bargain with me on the extras face-to-face: 'Will you knock a bit more off? Go on. Go on. She wants it this way. It's her wedding day.'

Most traveller men are respectful of me and treat me as a businesswoman, a bit of a female counterpart, I suppose, because their wives don't work. And, I have to say, I have always found the men easier to deal with. They are usually straightforward and will shake hands on things we've agreed, whereas the women will always come back later and ask for more even after we've agreed on everything. It's always, 'Oh, but can you do this for us, love? Will you just do that, it's only little.'

I had a woman in not long ago whose daughter's wedding we were working on. We'd already settled on what the dress would be like and agreed to do quite a lot of bridesmaids' dresses too. So she came in ready to pay and then asked me to 'throw in another couple of flower girls' dresses' at the very minute she was about to hand over the cash. I explained to her that I couldn't do them for nothing as they take ages to make, just like any other dress. 'Ah, but why not, love?' she asked, surprised. 'They're only little.'

The traveller women I deal with can be as bad as the girls when it comes to getting what they want. They can be manipulative and behave like children, and can turn the tears on at the drop of a hat, but I have to remind myself that they were only girls when they married and they've never done anything else in life but stay within their community and keep the home going.

The life in settled communities is very different in this way. When we leave home we generally go out to work, and I suppose that's when I started to grow up – because I was getting out in the world and meeting new people. By getting a chance to work with older, more experienced colleagues, I learned a lot about life. But life isn't like that for traveller women. They all just stay together every day, and without much outside influence on their lives they can be very childish.

Having said that, gypsy women have to deal with hardship; things that most people would hope to never have to go through in life. Lots of traveller families lose children because they are forced to live in temporary places that can be dangerous. They often park in car parks, or rat-infested, abandoned industrial sites, with the tops of their trailers just inches away from overhead cables. These are not ideal places to have kids running around, and it took me a while to get my head around the fact that travellers often live with none of the basic things that settled families are used to, like running water, electricity and access to healthcare.

A lot of the families we have had in the workshop talk about children of theirs that have died but, again, they do it in that strange, matter-of-fact way, or they may only mention it as part of another conversation. I always get the feeling that it's as if they expect it to happen, like it's a fact of life for them. It never ceases to surprise me, though, the practical way that gypsies deal with major life events, especially compared to the daft dramas they create over nothing.

But then gypsies always do things in their own way. The father lays down the rules for the family and they will be rules that his father taught him. Even in the workshop when we are fitting the girls' dresses, you'll hear the women saying to their daughters, 'Oh, your daddy won't like that,' or, 'I'll have to ask her daddy.' The dad always has the final word.

That's another thing about the gypsy way of life that I can relate to, because that's exactly how I was brought up. My dad was the head of the family and, no matter what, it was all down to 'your dad's word'. If I ever thought about getting into any sort of trouble when I was younger, the thing that was most likely to keep me in line was the thought that my dad would go through the roof if I did anything I wasn't supposed to. It was only when my mum started earning her own money that she had any say.

So, no wonder traveller girls don't drink, smoke or go with a boy on their own. These are unwritten rules in traveller society: girls remain protected until they are married. And no one protects them quite like their dad.

Some think that's a huge contradiction, because they will turn on *Big Fat Gypsy Weddings* and see little kids all dressed up, dancing and gyrating like Beyoncé. I know that the episodes showing weddings with the kids doing all that, with their spray-tans and make-up, shocked a lot of people. And I've got to hold my hands up here, because the first time me and Pauline saw these kids all dressed up and dancing provocatively for the cameras we couldn't believe it. I'll never forget it.

These two little girls walked in to the wedding party – they must have been eight or nine – with tiny mini-skirts and belly tops on. We were just horrified at what we were seeing. Paul turned to me and said, 'God, that's terrible. It's disgusting seeing kids dressed like that.' We didn't understand why anyone would let their kids dress up like that, in such an adult way, and it made us feel uncomfortable. But it's like everything that I've learned about the travellers' ways: a lot of it comes down to how you look at it.

One time a girl came to see me about making a wedding outfit for her four-year-old daughter. She asked for a big velvet skirt and a jacket with tails to match. But she wanted the jacket designed so that it didn't close, so you could see underneath it. Then she said, 'And I want a diamond bra.' The kid was four! But her next request was the most shocking of all: 'I want you to stuff it,' she said.

'Oh, no,' I said, 'I draw the line at that. I'm not doing that. If you want to put stuffing in the bra, then you do it, because I'm not putting it in.'

'No,' she said, 'I just want some padding in it. It's only like a bikini top.'

'I'll make you a bikini top,' I told her, 'but you couldn't go into a shop and buy a bikini top with stuffing in it for a four-year-old, so I'm not doing it.'

'But what's wrong with stuffing it?' she kept asking. She just didn't get my point. It wasn't wrong to her, and I realise now that that's because sexy clothes are like stage outfits to travellers, they're not about being sexy, more about being showy. I still refused to stuff the bra, though, because it was just not something I felt comfortable with.

The thing is, traveller kids love dancing and the parents love dressing their kids up like the TV pop idols they adore. They beam with pride when their children come out and do a show, just like my parents did when me and my brother performed on stage as kids. Except the stage for traveller kids is these parties. And all their adoring mums, dads and grannies will turn and watch. One little girl will come out and start dancing, and you think, 'That's sweet.' Then, within minutes, she'll just start really going for it and doing all these twisty moves like Shakira or Beyoncé – the gypsy girls idolise them – and you think, 'How the hell is that child moving her body like that?'

They are so good at all these dance moves – much better than anyone you see on the telly. So when the kids come out, everyone stops and says, 'You've got to watch this, it's amazing.' But there's always one standout kid who will keep going when all the others are finished, especially when the cameras are there. The families are really made up because that's one of their kids and they're really proud. It's just the kids showing off, and, as I always tell people, they're only copying what they've seen on telly.

The other guests also love watching the girls dance, because travellers just adore their children. And that means showering them with as much love and affection as they can. It's their nature to put the kids first and to give them the things that they think show how loved they are. I've been to Appleby horse fair – the yearly gathering of gypsies and travellers in Cumbria – and seen kids in prams glittering with crystals, with dummies hanging around their necks attached to solid gold chains.

And that's how life starts for a gypsy child: from the minute they are born these children are brought up to think, 'I am worth this and I am special.' Even the families that are not so well off, or who might not have all the money in the world, will just smother their children with affection. You can walk behind a traveller family and you'll hear a young lad of about 18 cooing to a child, 'Come on, my baby girl, come on, my baby girl.' They're always picking the kids up and hugging them. And the brothers and sisters are all so good and affectionate with their younger siblings. Traveller children are cosseted with love.

I often think about that when I talk to gypsy kids, and I'm always struck by how they beam with confidence. They're like little men and women, all very streetwise, and they will stand and talk to you and have a proper conversation without thinking about it. There's rarely any shyness, like there might be with other kids: it's totally natural for them to come and talk to you on your level. It's also natural that a lot of them don't read or write. But they're not embarrassed about it. Though I think more kids are being taught now.

Another difference I've noticed when working with traveller families and their kids is that the children interrupt adult conversations all the time. They are allowed to speak whenever they want. Whereas people in settled communities might say to their kids: 'Don't interrupt while I'm talking,' the travellers' attitude is more: 'My child's talking, so you have to listen.' The kids have this natural air of 'look at me, look at me'.

We have a lot of kids coming into the workshop for fittings and the little girls will always twirl around the floor when they put on a dress. They are only about two or three years old, but the women will be fawning over them, saying, 'Oh, look at you. You look like a princess. Wait till your sister sees you.' They give these kids confidence every step of the way, and I think that's why they all love their kids dressing up, so they can tell them how special they are.

But, saying that, the kids can be really rough with each other. I've seen a three-year-old smack a baby across the face quite hard. The baby started crying, but I didn't see the mother rush over and start chastising the three-year-old; she just picked the baby up off the floor and carried on talking.

You might see groups of kids happily playing together and then suddenly a big fight will break out and they'll start hitting each other. Or you might see young cousins from different families smacking each other. Now, that could cause murder between two families if it happened anywhere else, but it never seems to with travellers. Someone will just go and pull the kids away from each other. It's not dealt with in an emotional kind of way, the way I would probably deal with it. All these family ins and outs are handled without fuss, really.

Perhaps that's why traveller kids rarely cry. If one child kicks another, there's no whining. Unlike loads of kids today who seem to get away with crying at nothing, I've rarely seen a gypsy child moan. Even when they are all running around like mad at the weddings and falling over every two minutes, with their big bridesmaids' dresses on, they don't cry about hurting themselves.

Sometimes it looks as if they've been injured and you think, 'Oh God, is she OK?' but then they are up and running off again. These kids are just so tough, and I think that it's being brought up like that that makes the girls able to deal with the pain of wearing their heavy wedding dresses for up to twelve hours at a time. The gypsy girls can take a lot of pain if it means they are getting exactly what they want.

That's not to say that traveller kids are happy all the time or that they don't get frustrated like other children. If you watched *Big Fat Gypsy Weddings*, you're not likely to forget the episode where the little 11-year-old girl is upset because her sister's getting married and she knows that from that moment on she'll have to do all the family housework. In the show you see her having to bleach everything, everywhere. I can't imagine any kid being happy about that, and I have to say, having been in loads of caravans now, cleaning them from top to bottom every day does not look like an easy task. It must take hours and hours, as everything has to be spotless.

But gypsy women are not stuck in the house with their young children the way lots of women are. The whole family helps out. I visited a young mum with her newborn baby in a caravan once and she told me she had three other children, but her sister was looking after one and her mum had the other two, so it wasn't as bad as you might think. I've never known gypsy women to talk about suffering from things like post-natal depression, and I wonder if that's because they're always surrounded by their family and never left to cope on their own.

So, you see, though traveller women appear to be trapped in their communities in male-dominated marriages, they often also have a lot of freedom: if they want to go out for the day they can easily leave their kids with the family. As long as they are with their sisters or their mum, they can just go off and out without worrying, like most mums would.

I like that about traveller life – the fact that everyone keeps an eye on everyone else's kids; it means that they are free to play and if one runs off there will always be someone there who will go and bring them back. And think of all the weddings I've been to where it said on the invitation that children weren't allowed. Now, I'm not one to talk, because I didn't allow kids at my wedding – I didn't want them there because I was young and I wanted everything to be exactly how I wanted it, without children spoiling anything – but travellers would not go anywhere that their children are not allowed to go.

I think about how many of the children in settled communities seem to have no confidence. In my mind, the gypsy way shows that if you nurture a child and its personality, then that kid will grow up to think, 'I'm the best and I deserve the best, whatever the best might be.'

I'm always talking with the traveller women about their family lives, and I often ask them whether they'd like to change anything at all. I ask them if they'd like to give their teenagers a little more freedom to step out of the community, a chance to be more independent. And every single one of them, bar none, has come back with the same answer: 'No'.

14

The Tale of the Groom Who Was Nicked at the Altar

I've been working with travellers for fifteen years, been to hundreds of gypsy weddings and made thousands of gypsy dresses. In all that time, above all else, I've learned that working with gypsies is never, ever straightforward. And, really, that's one of the things I like about my job, because I never quite know what's going to happen next.

But one of the things I do know now – and which Gypsy Mary tried to teach me all those years ago at Paddy's, when I made my first wedding dress for her daughter – is that getting a straight answer to anything is nigh on impossible. Often it feels like no one is telling the truth. For example, it's not unusual for a customer to ask me to give them a bill for four times the amount of the actual cost of their dresses, just so they can show people what enormous amounts of money they are able to spend.

Coming up with these astronomical prices for the sake of their family pride doesn't do my business much good, though, as I get loads of Facebook messages saying things like, 'I'd love a dress made by you, but I don't have £50,000 to spend.'

But then a lot of what travellers say and do is simply about giving out messages that show others in the community how well they are doing. None of them will ever give you a clear idea of what is really going on. And because they will never tell me exactly what it is I need to know, I've got used to working a lot of it out for myself.

It didn't take me and Pauline long to notice that traveller weddings were quite different from the ones we usually got invited to. The first time we were asked to join the wedding party as guests was at one of the early weddings we did in Scotland for a bride called Sarah, who ended up being on TV on Sky's *Great British Weddings*. We were never that keen to join in before, usually because we were just so exhausted after fitting dresses. But we knew Sarah's family really well and they were adamant we should stay. So, after the wedding, we did as anyone would and followed everyone else on to the reception at the hotel.

But because travellers don't plan their weddings or send out invitations and there are no name places or allocated tables, or anything formal like that, when we got there we were just looking around wondering what to do next. One of the guests looked at us and could see that we were a bit lost, so she came over and said, 'Listen, love – when they open that door, run and stick your arse on a seat, because if you don't you won't get a meal.'

Pauline and me were a bit bewildered, so we just said, 'Right, OK,' and kept on moving towards the reception room. As we got there, the doors opened. Within seconds there was a stampede – women, kids, everyone just ran in and tried to get a seat as fast as they could. It was crazy. But everyone said the same: 'If you don't sit down you won't get a meal.' So all these people just threw themselves down wherever they could, and then stayed rigidly stuck to their seats until the meal was served.

'Bloody hell,' Pauline said as we watched everyone trying to stick their bums on seats. We just stood there taking it all in, trying to stop our jaws from dropping. It was weird to us then, but when we go to traveller weddings these days we know to go in and get a seat as soon as we can. It's normal to us now.

The other thing that was a real eye-opener was the way that some gypsies behaved during the church services. I was used to weddings where everyone sits in pews quietly waiting for the bride to arrive. If a guest's baby cries, or anything like that, they'll be hushed or taken out of the room, as a mark of respect to the couple, so that nothing spoils their special moment.

But at some traveller weddings we've been to, kids have been riding their bikes up and down the aisles, and in and out the pews, knocking everyone about. Pauline and me have often looked on, speechless. But we know now that all the raucous behaviour is quite normal, as no one makes any effort to calm things down.

Even funnier, often the priest just gets on with it, saying, 'Do you take this man …', while kids are running and screaming all over the place.

Then there was this other wedding we were invited to on the Wirral that was even more outrageous. We had finished fitting the bride's dresses and were seated in our pew for the ceremony. It was really noisy, as some of the kids had these little motorbikes that they were revving up outside while the service was going on. Other younger kids were coming in and out of the church with buckets of Kentucky Fried Chicken, sitting there eating it while the couple were saying their vows. It was pandemonium, all the screaming, shouting and running … the waft of takeaway chicken. It was more like being in a madhouse than a church.

And, because it was a Mass, it went on for well over an hour, and all the way through Pauline and me just sat there, looking at each other occasionally in disbelief, both thinking, 'What the hell is going on?' There were people shouting across the pews, all sorts – and it wasn't just the kids.

Then, just when we thought things couldn't get any more

out of control, the mother of the bride stood up and shouted, 'Now will youse all just shut the f*** up!'

Pauline looked at me and mouthed, 'Oh my God,' but the priest just carried on like it was nothing. We'd never seen a mother of a bride do that before! How would we ever forget it? But then there really are no rules at a gypsy wedding. All you can expect is the unexpected.

Travellers' reception parties are quite different too. One thing we noticed straight away was that the men and women don't sit together. There's a sense of, 'Why would you want to sit with your husband or wife when you've got your mates there?' And when the fellas do sit down, they all sit together, just tables and tables of men having a laugh.

Some of the other guests were a bit wary of Pauline and me when we first started going to traveller weddings, because we definitely weren't gypsies and lots of the guests didn't know who we were, as we hadn't worked with as many different traveller communities back then as we have now. There were a few who knew we made the wedding dresses, and some had worked with us since the Paddy's days, but travellers come to weddings from all over England and Ireland, and even from other countries, so there were a lot of people who weren't sure of us.

I suppose that we were seen as outsiders then. Some of the women seemed a bit hostile and they'd all turn their heads around in a 'What are you doing here?' kind of way. I think it was the way we dressed that made them wary, because we weren't glitzed up like they were. We were very much the odd ones out.

But little by little we became more accepted. Eventually people started coming over to us at the weddings and made a point of sitting down and talking to us. 'Are you the woman from Liverpool who makes the dresses?' they'd often ask. They all had lots of questions about the dresses, and we still get asked the same things now: how we make them, how long it takes, how much they cost and how can they place an order.

And now when we go to receptions, it's all, 'Can I have your phone number, love?' 'I'm so glad you're here as I've been trying to get your number for ages.' 'My brother's getting married. Can you make me something special?'

Customers often have trouble getting our number, because some travellers like to keep it secret from other families, as they don't want them to have clothes as nice or as special as the ones we have made for them. So they will tell anyone who asks for our number that they have lost it or don't know it. And it's not that easy for the families to find out more on the internet, as many of the travellers can't read or use a computer.

Now we've got plenty to talk about at the weddings, and more often than not we are treated like part of the family wherever we go. So much so that by the time we did *My Big Fat Royal Gypsy Wedding*, the TV special to coincide with the

Royal Wedding last April, the family asked me to organise the whole event.

It was one of the most stressful things I've ever done. So tough, in fact, that it reminded me of the time I made that first wedding dress for Gypsy Mary's daughter, with the 107-foot train. That nearly killed me, and it looked, at one point, as though this task would be the one to finally finish me off.

The wedding was in Peterborough and one of the reasons I think they were so keen for me to organise it was that they were having trouble getting a venue. That quickly turned into the first nightmare. Everywhere we asked said no; no one wanted to host a traveller wedding. Finally, one week before the Big Day, we managed to get a hall.

Only it was the community hall for a local charity for stray cats and dogs, an animal-rescue place. So when we got there, there were loads of dogs roaming around. Inside it was just a basic square room with a few tables in it and some old chairs stacked up in a corner. And there were pictures and stickers of cats and dogs stuck to the windows with yellowing Sellotape all over them. It looked bloody awful, to be honest, and I just stood there taking it all in, while the dogs were yelping and barking outside.

'Oh my God,' I muttered. 'What the hell are we going to do with this?'

But we had to go with it, as we couldn't organise anything else until we got the venue confirmed, so the pressure was really mounting. I just had to think of how best to turn it around – and how quickly I could manage it, too. Making Gypsy Mary's daughter's dress all those years ago was plain sailing in comparison.

Then I had a brainwave – we could just get one of those wedding marquee companies to come in and set up a marquee inside the room, and that's what we did. Then we set about making the interior look great.

Of course, things would not go the way I had planned them. I would never have expected them to, but I was really adamant that the reception room should look lovely, just the way I wanted. So, an hour or so before the wedding, I went in to check that everything was OK. It looked fantastic – the top table, everything; it was all done. I was really happy.

But after the church service, when the guests came in after the wedding, all these men just went and sat at the top table before the bride and groom had even come in.

I don't know what made me think that the travellers were going to start behaving like they would at a non-traveller wedding, because that's not their way – and I should know that better than anyone – but I was just so keen to make the wedding the best I could. There were about 400 guests coming in and, to me, it was pretty obvious that that was the top table, so I couldn't believe these men just thought it was OK to go and plonk themselves down at it. I was just looking at them all and thinking, 'You've just spoilt the whole thing sitting down there. I'm not having this.' So I went over to them and said, 'Excuse me, are you the mother and father of the bride?'

This fella just looked at me and said, 'No, I'm her uncle.'

'Well, do you think you could move to another table?' I said. 'There are loads of other tables, and this is for her dad and her mum and people like that.'

'Oh, is it?' he said and got up to move.

But no sooner had he left and I'd turned my back than another fella sat down in the same place. In the end I just had to stand there like a guard, telling everyone, 'You can't sit here. No, you can't sit here …' Everyone was just sitting down where the hell they wanted. No one cared about anything like that. Except me. But then I'm still used to my own friends' and family's weddings being very formal, where it's all, 'Let's be upstanding for the bride and groom,' and everyone sits around making small talk.

Traveller weddings have absolutely no rules and you honestly never know what's going to happen next. There really are no limits. I don't mind being a guest at one but I don't think I'll be rushing to organise another one any time soon.

A few years ago, me and Pauline were at another big wedding near Birmingham, where the bride was a lovely girl called Bonnie. We were in a hotel room fitting her dress ready to go to church when someone came in and told us that the police had turned up there. To arrest the groom!

We gasped. Bonnie started crying. We knew we had to get her to the church as soon as we could to see what was going on.

When we got there the coppers had put the groom in handcuffs. All the women were screaming at them, 'You can't do that! He's just about to get married!' I just stood there watching it all, shocked.

Eventually they agreed to let the wedding go ahead, but the groom had to remain handcuffed, and Bonnie kept crying. But the vicar went ahead, and so, with the groom in handcuffs and the bride sobbing, Bonnie and her groom were married. When the service was over the guests headed to the reception, and she went with her new husband to the police station where he was being held for questioning. It was quite sad really. Then a couple of hours later she was back at the reception enjoying her wedding party, as if nothing had happened.

I remember that we had been asked to do Bonnie's wedding in double-quick time, so at first I'd wondered if maybe she was pregnant. She didn't seem to be, but it always crosses my mind that something's up when we are asked to do a wedding really quickly.

We never found out why they arrested her husband – it didn't seem right to ask, and no one told us – but the rumours at the wedding were that her husband had set up the arrest so that he didn't have to marry her. They can't have been true, though, because it was obvious this fella loved Bonnie and they're really happily married now.

While no one wants the police to turn up at their wedding, gypsy weddings are unusual in that anyone is allowed to turn up to them. There's never any set list of invitees, and so you'll often get some guests coming who have an ongoing spat with another family, sometimes even if it's the bride's. But gypsies think it's disrespectful not to invite someone, regardless of the fact that they might not want certain people to be there, so instead they just don't send any invites.

But while they wouldn't turn another family away, this is one of the other reasons for them being so secretive about where and when their weddings are happening – sometimes they don't want certain parts of the family to know, in case there is trouble. So dates will be swapped, venues will be changed, and no one will have any idea of what is really going on. That's why finding your way to a gypsy wedding often comes down to word of mouth.

And traveller women love to talk – it's like the bush tele-graph, and they'll tell you everything that's going on. So you can usually get a good idea of what is happening from them, even if they are all giving you different versions of the same story. Whatever happens in that community, if you know the right people, you'll know about it within around fifteen minutes of it going on. Honestly, it's that quick.

One of the things that I know traveller women talk about a lot is our Hit List. They are always asking us who is on it. We started the Hit List a few years back when we decided that there were some families and people that we were just not prepared to work with any more. I mean, we have learned to work around most travellers' ways, such as the bargaining and the constant mind-changing. We are fine with all that. But there are customers who have just pushed us to the limits and given us the run-around too many times, so their names go on the Hit List. Whenever anyone calls, everyone knows to check the List, which is pinned in a secret place in the office, and to hand the phone over to Pauline or me if the person on the other end of the line is one of the names on it.

This one family, who ended up on the Hit List, had come over from Belfast to pick up a wedding's worth of outfits – flower girls' dresses, bridesmaids' dresses, pageboy suits, the lot. Everything was ready, but when the woman came in, she decided that she wanted some extra decoration on the outfits, including six cravats and hankies and long gloves for all the bridesmaids. She also wanted alterations and asked for two of the dresses to be made shorter. In typical traveller style, she also said that she wanted them done that day so that she could take them back to Ireland with her that night.

Now this family had been on the Hit List before. Back then they had asked us to make an engagement outfit for their daughter. When the mother came to pick it up she said that she wanted to change the style of skirt and have some more decoration added, even though we had designed the dress exactly as she had ordered it – I showed her the original sketch we did to prove it.

'Yes, I know that's what I asked for then,' she said. 'But I've changed my mind and now I want more diamanté on it and something for her hair as well.'

'We can't do this all in a night,' I told her.

She started crying. 'Oh please do it, Thelma, please.'

'We can't do these changes for you tonight,' I told her. 'We just can't do all the things you want by nine o'clock.'

So her husband comes in and asks me, 'If we stay the night in Liverpool, can you make the dresses with all the extra details ready to pick up tomorrow?'

'OK,' I said. 'Fine. Come back tomorrow and we'll have it done for you.' Of course, this meant that we would have to stay and work most of that night, which we do a lot. But we are sometimes OK to do that if we know that a family has travelled from Ireland and needs to go back the next day. I'm also really keen that my customers leave knowing that they have the very best.

So we stayed that night, even though we were shattered, having worked late the night before. While we were working on the changes, Pauline told me she remembered the woman coming in and that she'd been a bit of a nightmare customer from the off. 'That's it,' she said. 'First thing in the morning they are going on the Hit List. In fact, she's going to the top.'

To this day, I do not know how they managed to slip off the List unnoticed. Nobody in the workshop ever admitted to taking their wedding order. But here she was up to her old tricks again.

At one point some of the girls were actually starting to fall asleep, and we still had so much left to do. So Pauline kept up with the coffees. But when we got into the wee small hours everyone slumped again, so Pauline decided the only way forward was to take action with some Pro-Plus and Red Bull.

We were all so tired and delirious, but there was a lot left to do. And, I'll tell you what, we didn't half get the work done after Pauline did her rounds. Through the night she dished out constant supplies of caffeine, in various forms. By the end everyone was buzzing.

So, laughing away and doing silly pranks, we worked right the way through, and at about nine o'clock the next morning the couple came back to collect everything. Now, had it all gone smoothly that would have been fine. But you can imagine just how exhausted we were – I could hardly speak I was so tired. And what I really didn't need was any of the usual to-ing and fro-ing, when they knew how hard we had had to work to give them all the extras they wanted so they could get back to Ireland in time.

But they were delighted. So Pauline and the girls started to pack everything up ready for them to take back to Ireland, while the husband came into the office with me to settle the bill.

Now, I'd only charged him something like £300 extra for all the other bits, so there was really nothing he could quibble about.

'What's that?' he said, pointing to the bill.

'That's for the extras that your wife wanted,' I said.

'Well, I'm not going to pay that,' he said. 'I haven't got that and you said it was going to be this much, not that much.'

'Yeah, but yesterday your wife came in and said she wanted all these other bits,' I said to him. It was like talking to a brick wall. He wasn't listening. He didn't want to listen. So he called his wife in. And then she started.

'What's this for?' she asked. 'What are you charging me for that for?'

'All these extras that you asked for yesterday,' I told her. My blood was beginning to boil. 'We all stayed here working the whole of last night to do these,' I said.

'We don't care what you've done,' she snapped.

I was livid. 'Do you know what?' I screamed at them. 'Just keep your money and get the hell out of here!'

I was so tired. I was sick to my back teeth looking at them. In fact, I just couldn't look at them any more. But he was still going on and on. Pauline had heard me screaming all over the factory, so she came into the office.

'You heard her,' she said. 'Now *get* out!'

They still kept saying, 'No, no, no.'

'I can't even look at you,' I screamed.

Pauline managed to get rid of them in the end, and we got our money plus the £300 they said they didn't have, but it was an absolute nightmare.

After that incident with the all-nighter, the woman called up a few months later and said to Pauline, 'Have I done something to offend you?' She had wanted us to do an outfit for her and had been calling quite a lot but we hadn't been returning her calls because she was such a pain.

'All I know,' said Pauline, 'is that you are on the List.'

'You don't have to explain to her,' I said to Pauline. 'It's enough to say we're busy.'

But Pauline said this woman wanted to talk to me, so I phoned her up. 'Hi, it's Thelma,' I said.

'Oh, hiya.'

'Listen, before you go any further,' I told her, 'you asked Pauline if we had a problem with you. Well, yeah, we do have a problem,' I said.

'But why?' she asked. 'Why? I *thought* you were being funny with me.'

'No one's being funny with you,' I told her. 'It's just that we'll never do anything for any of you again.'

'Why?'

'Well, were you not there when we had all that drama over the cost of the extras on the wedding outfits?' I asked her.

'But you got your money,' she said.

'Yeah, but you really pushed us right to the edge,' I told her. 'You already caused a scene over the engagement outfit and this is just another drama that we don't want to deal with.'

'Oh, I'm so, so sorry,' she said. 'I'm so sorry, Thelma.' And on and on she went. But I told her that she was on the Hit List and that was that. Over the next couple of weeks she sent cards. Then she sent flowers. She sent everything. So we took her off the Hit List in the end, but I warned her that if she behaved like that again our relationship with her family would be over for good.

The families hate the idea of being on the Hit List, because they all want the best dresses and if we don't do them people know. Only last week we had a call from a girl whom we had made outfits for a year before. At the last minute the wedding was called off, so we were left with a whole load of clothes that we had made for the people who were meant to be going who never came to pick them up.

So, here's this girl on the phone a year later and she's getting married again, and she says she wants to come and get the dresses. Only she's pregnant now and says that the dress we made for her won't fit. She wanted us to alter it for nothing, but Pauline told her that that wasn't our fault and she could either come and pick the dresses up or leave them.

She told Pauline she'd be coming on the Saturday to pick everything up. But Pauline told her she couldn't come that day as we had a couple of wedding fittings on. But she was adamant that she was coming, so I had to lay down the law with her: 'Listen, you can't come on Saturday, end of story. You can come on Monday.'

She didn't turn up on the Monday and there was still no sign of her by Tuesday. This was annoying, at such a busy time, and so I told Pauline to phone her and get an exact time that she was going to come in. When Pauline got her on the line she said she didn't want them.

'Tell her not to come to us ever again and that she's on the List and that's it,' I said. So about two hours later this girl called Pauline back saying that she was really sorry and that she had been arguing with her husband at the time, and that she would be down the next day to pick them up.

'OK then, that's fine,' I said.

'Oh, and she wants to know if she can come off the List,' Pauline said.

'Yeah, all right, take her off,' I said.

And she came and picked everything up.

There are around fifty names on the Hit List, but there is one woman who is at the top and she will never, ever get off. This woman's daughter's wedding was cancelled about three days before it was meant to take place. So she called and said that she wanted her money back and that she was coming down to the workshop the next day to get it.

'Er, no,' I said, 'we can't give you the money back because everything's been done. Your dress is here ready for you to collect.'

So she started screaming down the phone, giving me abuse, and I'm talking absolute abuse. 'You don't know who I am,' she screamed. 'I'm going to come and burn your shop down and I'm going to …' On and on she went.

Then she came down to the workshop the next day with her daughter, Angeline, who we knew quite well as we'd spent weeks with her making the dress. And there were a few other girls from the family with her as well.

So, the mum came in to see me and kept barking, 'I want my money. I'm going to burn this shop down. Give me my money.'

She was scary – but I'd just had enough. 'Who do you think you're talking to?' I said. 'Do you think I stood on Paddy's Market for years so that the likes of you could come in here and speak to me like that?'

'You don't know who I know,' she came back again.

'Don't you threaten me,' I said to her. 'Don't you dare!'

She softened a bit: 'Oh, I know, love, but what am I going to do? I need the money.'

'Look,' I said, 'can't you get it in your head that it's not our fault? We didn't call the wedding off.'

'Oh, I know, love, but I've got no money.'

'Well, if I give you the money back then *I'll* have no money,' I said. 'She's bound to get asked for again, so we will keep the dress here.' She left it in the end, but she was intimidating and I hope that she doesn't come back. I'll let anyone off the List if they behave, but not her.

I don't bow down to bullies, and I've also got Pauline on my team. And Pauline doesn't take any nonsense from anyone. That includes me. Pauline goes mad at me sometimes over the way I charge for the dresses. She says I put too low a price on everything. And she's not afraid to say it in front of the customers either, especially when they just keep adding more and more to the order.

So, the mums will all be asking whether I can just do this and do that, after we've agreed the price, and more often than not I'll say, 'Yeah, go on then.'

But Pauline won't have it. 'Well, do you know what, Thelma?' she'll say. 'You might as well just give it away. We'll all have no jobs next year, that's what we'll have.' She'll just sit there looking at me, as if to say, 'You idiot!' It's like good cop, bad cop with Paul and me. I'm the good one, she's the bad one. She just will not have their messing around, and they know it.

If the customers really play up, Pauline will think nothing about throwing them out. A year or so ago we'd done another late night and this woman was quibbling about the money for her daughter's engagement dress for hours and hours. In the end Pauline just threw her and her family out, locked the door, and said they could keep all their money and go home because she'd had enough. They were all outside banging on the back door trying to get back in. So I said to the girls in the workshop, let's leave them to it and go out and get some breakfast, just to get away from the noise apart from anything else. So we all filed quietly out the front and left them banging on the door round the back while we had some breakfast in the café across the road.

Pauline was still bristling about it. 'What are we going to do with that dress? It's not going to fit anyone. And what about that colour? Oh no!'

'I bet they'll still be there banging on the door when we get back,' I said. And they were. Almost an hour later.

'I'm sorry, I'm sorry,' the woman was saying. And you know, she came up with the money in the end, but it was too little too late. She's phoned so many times since asking us to make other outfits, but she's on the Hit List now, and Pauline says she's not coming off it any time soon.

15

The Tale of What Happened Next

Looking back, I think it was Margaret's wedding dress that really started it all off for us. Because she was barely an adult, but was allowed to get anything she wanted, her dress was on a completely different scale to anything we'd done before. No one had ever seen anything like it, including us, so that dress started a phenomenon, and I think that's what made people so fascinated by traveller weddings. I think there was a curiosity as to why the dresses were so gigantic, and people were intrigued about the travellers obviously spending a lot of money on them.

So perhaps it was no surprise that after Margaret's 21-stone dress appeared in the local paper, I had the world's press knocking at my door, including TV stations from America to Australia, wanting to talk to both me and Margaret.

The press knew that I had made the dress, but the other reason they were all so keen to get me on the phone was that Margaret didn't want to talk to anyone. There was just no way they would be able to track her down. It took me years to be able to get in touch with travellers on the phone, and even longer to gain their trust, so there was no way the media was going to have any joy overnight. And it's been like that ever since – I can get through to lots of travellers where others can't. Now I have direct telephone numbers for most of the families.

So when they couldn't get in touch with Margaret they knew that one person who might be able to was me. 'Would she come on *This Morning*?' I was asked. But Margaret was adamant and said she would never do any interviews. They kept offering her a lot of money to talk, and I used to laugh, thinking, 'Money – you've no idea. That's the last thing that girl wants.'

Not long after that, a TV production company got in touch with me. They were making a show called *Britain's Youngest Brides* for ITV and asked us if we would talk to one of the girls we were making a dress for at the time to see if she wanted to be on it. There were going to be five weddings on it, including a young Indian girl's arranged marriage, and they wanted a traveller wedding too.

The thing was that we had taken part in a programme called *Great British Weddings* for Sky TV a couple of years earlier, which had featured one of our traveller brides.

When it was on TV the bit about our girl, Sarah, really stood out. It was all coming across really well. Then, right at the end of the clip of her getting married, they showed a fight breaking out.

I was really disappointed by that and wished they hadn't done it. That wasn't the point of the programme, was it? It was a cheap shot. 'Do you know what?' I said to Pauline. 'There was no need to put that in.' I was a bit disillusioned with what they'd done there, because up until then it was good. That experience made me wary about dealing with TV people and their motivations for asking us to get the gypsies involved in their programmes. I didn't trust them.

But a bride we were doing a dress for at the time was really keen to take part, so we ended up giving TV another chance. They didn't show any fights on the ITV programme, but I still wasn't really happy – I just felt they weren't showing travellers in the best light.

Yet, when the dresses were on TV, my phone would ring off the wall with media people wanting to talk to me. I wasn't that interested then, though, because of my past experiences.

Mostly I didn't even take their calls, but there was this one guy, Neil, who actually lived on the Wirral and said he had a production company. He knew about me and came to see me at the workshop. 'I've got this idea about doing a story about the dresses for television,' he said. 'Can I come back and do a little bit of filming with you?' He lived locally, so I said, 'Yeah, OK.' He seemed like a nice guy, even though he was a little bit overbearing at times and would come and hang about the workshop a bit too long.

He kept coming in and filming and promising us that he would get a TV company to take on the story. I was still a bit wary about it though, because filming is very time-consuming and I knew I couldn't afford to take lots of time away from the business.

In the meantime another production company, Firecracker, called me. The producer, Jenny Popplewell, said that they were also interested in talking to me about doing a documentary on travellers and their weddings.

'Can I come and meet you?' she asked.

'Let me see when I've got time,' I said, but never thought much more of it and didn't get back to her. But Jenny wouldn't leave it and phoned me almost every month for six months. I'd always tell the girls in the workshop to say that I wasn't there.

So Jenny stopped calling me for a while and Neil was taking forever to get anything done, so I just forgot about the whole telly thing. Then one day I answered the phone and it was Jenny again. She just said, 'Hiya, it's Jenny.' After a while I said, 'Do you know what? You're so persistent, just come and do it.'

The following Saturday Jenny came down with her cameraman to start filming what they call a 'taster', a short video sample of what the show might be, that they can use to pitch the idea to TV companies. That show was *Big Fat Gypsy Weddings*, which was to become one of the most popular and talked-about British documentary TV series of the past few years. And a show that I was to be a regular part of.

I liked Jenny straight away, especially as she said that her idea did not involve ridiculing the travellers and their way of life – a point that I had stressed to her.

I trusted her, she was different, and I've grown to like her so much that I even call her 'daughter number four'. She kept her word about everything she promised me at the start, and the travellers love her and trust her now too. Who knows, if it wasn't for Jenny, *Big Fat Gypsy Weddings* might never have been made.

And my life has changed a lot since Jenny and the cameras arrived that Saturday. With the programme being such a big hit, I now get recognised a lot in the street. We've got loads of fans of the dresses from all over the world following us on Twitter and Facebook now. Recently we even had this fella in who had travelled all the way from New Zealand to see us. They'd shown the series on TV there and this guy was so hooked that he came to Liverpool especially to see the shop and the dresses.

He rang us the day he arrived, and he was in luck as we had a massive dress on the stand that was going to be shown at an exhibition. So this New Zealand fella came over to the workshop to see it with three friends in tow. 'He honestly looked like he was going to have a heart attack when he saw the dress,' Pauline said to me after they'd gone. 'He was in raptures!' He just kept saying, 'Thank you so much!' and hugging her. I was really touched and so I tweeted it: 'This sweet guy has just come all the way from New Zealand to see the dresses. Thought he was going to hyperventilate!' And I got loads of replies back from America, saying, 'Why not? We wanna see you over here. We love you in America.' I was just like, 'Oh my God!' I still can't believe the response to our dresses.

Even my friends say to me, 'Oh, how does it feel to be a celebrity now?' But that makes me laugh because, really, I just do what I do. I'm a dressmaker. I admit that I do get recognised in the street a lot more these days, but I'm not a celebrity. Maybe I was just in the right place at the right time.

And there are other dressmakers working with the traveller communities, and making wedding dresses for them, so I'm not the only person who does it.

Sometimes, though, I do think about why things have worked out the way they have. I suppose that I have always felt a natural affinity with my gypsy customers, since they first started coming to see me and that woman asked me to make these *Gone With the Wind* dresses all these years ago at Paddy's. I also think that I feel an empathy with the young girls whose lives remind me of so many elements of my young life.

Getting married young is so very important to them, in the way it was for me, because it allows them to escape the control of the family and branch out on their own. So I look at all the 15- and 16-year-old girls that we work with and sometimes I can see myself in them, all wrapped up in the idea of getting married.

But every gypsy girl who comes to me looking for a dress presents a different challenge. You are introduced to a family and then you realise that they are related to another customer and that they have loads more relatives that you never even knew about, and wouldn't make the connection with, as they seem so different to the family members we've got to know.

Looking back to when I first started working with travellers, that's what they were to me – just travellers – but now I know masses of individual characters and personalities and understand so much more about the different traveller communities.

I think I have struck up my closest friendships with the Irish gypsies, as these are the ones I know more. They are so open and warm and are always running in and out of the workshop, dying to talk to me and tell me everything that's going on. Other gypsy communities are a bit more private about the goings-on in their lives.

Rathkeale travellers are very protective and don't want to bring attention to their community. But I'm fascinated by the way the Rathkeale families do things, so I'll talk to their girls whenever I can and ask about their customs.

'Who decides how much dowry someone gets?' I asked one of the girls.

'Oh, that's just between the families,' she said.

'Is it the uglier the girl, the more of a dowry a family has to pay?' I asked, having a laugh.

'No, it's not like that. Not at all,' she laughed. 'There are plenty of pretty girls whose families have had to pay large dowries too.'

The Romanies and the English gypsies are completely different again. A few of the Romanies are still not that happy about how gypsy life was portrayed in the Channel 4 TV series, or about having their communities exposed. And I still get messages from a few of them saying that I am not representing travellers in the right way. But I tell them that I am not a representative for the gypsy community – I am a dressmaker.

But the one thing that I love most about all the travellers is their history and their strong sense of community. The gypsies have got that strength of family feeling that means their kids have always got someone to go to. I remember when I was a kid I felt a bit isolated at times and wanted more people I could relate to. My favourite thing was being at my grandma's house, because all my cousins would be there and we'd all come together. I was just desperate to be part of a bigger family. I think my mum only had the two of us because she wanted to give my brother and me everything, which she wouldn't have been able to do if she'd had more kids.

Also, like traveller parents, my mum and dad spent their lives instilling a huge amount of confidence in us. From day one my parents brought me up to feel like I was the most special kid in the world. Whatever I wanted, I never heard my mum say no to us, ever. She'd kill herself to make sure we got what we wanted.

And, when I was young, my dad would always say to me, 'Would I ever let anything hurt you? Nothing bad will ever happen to you.' I thought my dad was the best man since time began. Other kids at school would talk about their dads and I'd think to myself, 'But you don't know *my* dad.' Of course, he was just an ordinary fella, but to me he could make things happen and he always taught me that second best is no good; you've always got to strive to be the best.

That's why I think all this stuff that people tell their kids today – that it's all about the taking part – is a load of rubbish. My dad taught me that you've got to go for what you want. And my mum did the same: 'Just deal with what you've got,' she always said to me. 'It doesn't matter what anyone throws at you.'

So, like the traveller girls, ever since I was born I have done everything to get my parents' approval. I always wanted my mum to say, 'I'm proud of you' – but she's never ever said it. But last year she was in hospital and one of the nurses said to her, 'I know your face from somewhere.' She asked if it was from such-and-such a place. Then she said, 'I think I know you off the telly!'

'I've not been on the telly,' my mum said, 'but my daughter's the dressmaker in *Big Fat Gypsy Weddings*.' And then told her all about the programme. So the nurse got very excited and called all the other nurses and doctors over to meet her. They gathered around and were asking my mum to tell them everything about the show. The next time I saw my mum she said, 'I walked out of hospital feeling ten feet tall.'

'I can't believe you just said that you were proud of me,' I told her.

'I'm proud of both of my kids,' she said. I cried my eyes out all the way home.

A week later I took the draft of the first chapter of this book for her to read. She read about two lines and then carried on playing with baby Phoebe, my Hayley's daughter. 'Have you read that, Mum?' I said.

'Oh, I'll read it in a minute,' she said.

So it was back to normal: 'Just get on with it!'

I really do believe that life is all about how you see and deal with things. I got through my time in prison because I saw it differently to how my friend Donna did. Donna found the whole thing really hard and went into herself, staying in her cell alone at night. She was depressed, like a lot of women in prison – they're all on anti-depressants – but I wouldn't allow it to depress me. I made the best of what it was by going to the gym, getting fit, learning how to use the computer. I knew that when I came out at the other end these things would help me; that there were other things to do. So I really think you can do all you want in life if you approach it in the right way. And I think I've lived to tell the tale.

When I first started working with Firecracker, I told them straight away about my time in prison, as I don't feel I have anything to hide and I thought that they should know in case it caused problems for them.

That up-front way is something else I'd say I have in common with the travellers. I think being in prison is quite normal to them – a lot of gypsy men end up in prison. So they talk about being inside in a matter-of-fact way. It's not unusual for the young girls who we are making dresses for to cut a fitting short because they have got to go and visit their partner or brother in prison.

In fact, I've been talking to a young traveller girl who is interested in coming to work with us as a trainee. She's the sister of a girl we're doing a wedding dress for. She's always talking to us about how much she loved going to school.

She's an intelligent kid, and she's really keen to start working for me and to go to college. Just the other day she was on her way out of the workshop when she stopped and came back. 'Would it make any difference if I've been in trouble?' she asked me, nervously.

I looked at her. 'No, it wouldn't,' I said.

'I've been locked up,' she said.

'Don't worry about it, love,' I said. 'Haven't we all!'

Looking back, when I split up with Kenny I was 39 or 40, and I thought that that part of my life was over and that I'd never meet someone again. Then I met Dave and I suddenly felt, 'Is this what it's supposed to be like when you're with someone?' He adores my family, and seeing him with my kids, and the way he was there for them when I was in prison, made me love him even more. And it just gets better and better. He's a rock. We have also got a daughter, Katrina, and Dave is as brilliant a dad as I imagined he would be.

Then I think about how everything started, fifteen years ago, on Paddy's Market and the way that the business has grown, and how the travellers and the dresses we make for them are such a big part of my life.

That's why, when the gypsy girls come in for the last fitting, to see their finished wedding dress, we always do this little performance. We put a screen across the door and then open it to let the bride walk in first. I love that moment, but I still get knots in my stomach before they walk through. Sometimes the girl will walk in and say nothing, and we'll all look at each other as if to say, 'Oh no!'

'Do you like it?' I'll say.

'Oh, I love it. I just love it,' she'll reply.

Of course, lots of the girls are too overwhelmed to speak, and usually they start crying at that point. The mums are always so, so proud: 'You've never done a dress like this before, have you, love? Have you?' they'll ask me.

'Oh, no, never one like that,' I say.

Then the bride has to try the dress on, and we send the rest of her family away for half an hour while we get her dressed. When they come back, we put the girl in the middle of the floor and turn all the lights off except for one – a spotlight above her head. Then we open the door. The mum usually starts crying and all the young kids rush in and start dancing around the bride saying, 'Put the music on,' or 'Come on, let's see her dance in it.'

Every time we finish a dress, I stand there and look at this really young kid so excited and happy, and every time I think the same thing: Thelma Madine, you have the loveliest job in the world.

Acknowledgements

I attribute very little of my success to myself, because it is the people around me who give me the ability to do what I do.

First and foremost, a big thank you to Leanne, Yanli, Stacey and all my other fantastic Nico staff, for helping me along the path that has led to this high point in my career. With a special thank you to my best friend Pauline for sticking by me through thick and thin, and playing a massive part in the successes of Nico.

Thank you to Mary Hogan, Mary Hughes, Josie Berger and all my other mates from Paddy's Market for your support over the years and the wonderful ability you all had to make me laugh when things got really tough.

I am so grateful to Hayley Rios, Laura Lees, Julie MacBrayne and all of the rest of the team at HarperCollins for giving me the opportunity to write this book. I'm especially grateful to Vicky McGeown for encouraging me throughout, seeing to it that my story was told and participating in every stage of its production.

A special thanks also to Caragh McKay for your patience and painstaking proofreading of the text.

I am indebted to Tina and Liam at Channel 4 for seeing the potential in *Big Fat Gypsy Weddings* and for believing in me.

I also want to thank everybody at Firecracker Films: Jes, Vicky, Jack, Osca, Daniel, Sam, Morag, Julie, Guy, Lizzie, Ben, Lawrence, Laura, Rachel, Aaron, Emily, Nick, Zoe, Max and Cathy for your continued support. I'd like to thank Sue Oriel for always being at the other end of the phone, advising and guiding me through every step and helping to turn my dreams of writing this book into a reality. And a big thank you to Jenny Popplewell – your gentle powers of persuasion started me on this incredible journey.

Last, but certainly not least, the biggest thanks goes to my amazing family. First to Dave for helping me turn my life around, for your support – both emotional and financial – for loving me unconditionally, but most of all for believing in me. I'd like to thank my children and my grandchildren for understanding that when my to-do lists piled higher and higher I couldn't give you as much of my time as I would have liked.

Most importantly I would like to thank my mum and dad, Thelma and Leo Makin. Your constant support and nurturing is the reason all of this was possible. Mum, you are my driving force. You showed me the value of hard work and it is you who inspired me to be passionate in what I do. To hear you say that you are proud of me is my ultimate reward.

Picture Credits

Section 1: page 4, top left: courtesy of the *Peterborough Evening Telegraph*; page 4, bottom right: © *Liverpool Echo*; page 5, top left: © South West News Service

Section 2: page 2, top left: © South West News Service

All other images courtesy of the author.